Chess

Teach Yourself VISUALLY™

Chess

Visual®

by Jon Edwards

BICENTENNIAL
1807
WILEY
2007
BICENTENNIAL

Wiley Publishing, Inc.

Teach Yourself VISUALLY™ Chess

Copyright © 2007 by Wiley Publishing, Inc., Hoboken, New Jersey. All rights reserved.

Published by Wiley Publishing, Inc., Hoboken, New Jersey

For general information on our other products and services or to obtain technical support please contact our Customer Care Department within the U.S. at (800) 762-2974, outside the U.S. at (317) 572-3993 or fax (317) 572-4002.

Wiley also publishes its books in a variety of electronic formats. Some content that appears in print may not be available in electronic books. For more information about Wiley products, please visit our web site at www.wiley.com.

Library of Congress Control Number: 2006926120

ISBN-13: 978-0-470-04983-9
ISBN-10: 0-470-04983-9

Printed in the United States of America

10   9   8   7   6   5   4   3   2   1

Book production by Wiley Publishing, Inc. Composition Services

Praise for the Teach Yourself VISUALLY Series

I just had to let you and your company know how great I think your books are. I just purchased my third Visual book (my first two are dog-eared now!) and, once again, your product has surpassed my expectations. The expertise, thought, and effort that go into each book are obvious, and I sincerely appreciate your efforts. Keep up the wonderful work!

—Tracey Moore (Memphis, TN)

I have several books from the Visual series and have always found them to be valuable resources.

—Stephen P. Miller (Ballston Spa, NY)

Thank you for the wonderful books you produce. It wasn't until I was an adult that I discovered how I learn—visually. Although a few publishers out there claim to present the material visually, nothing compares to Visual books. I love the simple layout. Everything is easy to follow. And I understand the material! You really know the way I think and learn. Thanks so much!

—Stacey Han (Avondale, AZ)

Like a lot of other people, I understand things best when I see them visually. Your books really make learning easy and life more fun.

—John T. Frey (Cadillac, MI)

I am an avid fan of your Visual books. If I need to learn anything, I just buy one of your books and learn the topic in no time. Wonders! I have even trained my friends to give me Visual books as gifts.

—Illona Bergstrom (Aventura, FL)

I write to extend my thanks and appreciation for your books. They are clear, easy to follow, and straight to the point. Keep up the good work! I bought several of your books and they are just right! No regrets! I will always buy your books because they are the best.

—Seward Kollie (Dakar, Senegal)

Credits

Acquisitions Editor
Pam Mourouzis

Project Editor
Donna Wright

Technical Editor
Richard Benjamin

Editorial Manager
Christina Stambaugh

Publisher
Cindy Kitchel

Vice President and Executive Publisher
Kathy Nebenhaus

Interior Design
Kathie Rickard
Elizabeth Brooks

Cover Design
José Almaguer

Photography
Matt Bowen

Photographic Assistant
Andrew Hanson

About the Author

Jon Edwards is a four-time winner of the American Postal Chess Tournaments (APCT) championship and a two-time winner of the APCT Game of the Year award. He won the United States Correspondence Chess Championship in 1997 and the North American Invitational Correspondence Chess Championship in 1999. He became an International Master in 1997 and a Senior International Master in 1999. Jon is currently competing on the U.S. Correspondence Chess Olympiad Team. His ICCF rating of 2,580 places him in top 200 correspondence chess players in the world.

Jon is also the webmaster of Chess is Fun (www.queensac.com), a site that provides free chess instruction. He has authored seven chess books, including *The Chess Analyst,* (Thinkers Press, 1997), which chronicled his success in the U.S. Championship.

He is a 1975 graduate of Princeton University, where he serves today as the Coordinator of Institutional Communications and Outreach within the Office of Information Technology. He resides in Pennington, New Jersey, with his wife Cheryl and two sons, Aaron and Neil.

Acknowledgments

I want to thank Wiley Publishing for the opportunity to write this book. As a chess teacher for more than 30 years, I have seen the importance of chess in young peoples' lives. While almost all players come to enjoy the game as a worthwhile pursuit and simply a whole lot of fun, in my experience, some players come to understand the game better than others. The reason, I believe, has much to with the different styles of learning. A few of my students are comfortable memorizing long sequences but, by and large, most prefer to learn the game visually, through pattern recognition and by learning to identify the various visual clues on the board.

I have tried throughout this book to provide an introduction to and discussion of chess in a way that I believe is pedagogically sound for visual learners. These are the basic lessons that I have provided to young and old for decades. Wiley has assisted the effort in a very important way by producing a book with high-quality photographs of the board. Almost all chess books use diagrams that look straight down on the chessboard and represent the pieces with symbols. Here, you will see the board as it exists and from an angle that promotes understanding as well as excellent posture.

It is fitting that a book like this should have such an amazing photograph of the author. Special appreciation goes to Princeton University's photographer Denise Applewhite for her impressive skill.

The editors at Wiley are a very professional bunch and throughout made my life an easier one. Pam Mourouzis understood the importance of this book from the beginning. I thank her also for her willingness to bend her deadlines around my work schedule. Editors Donna Wright and Christina Stambaugh helped to shape the book into its current form. They know their craft and pursue it with impressive dedication. I am also grateful for the excellent technical editing job that Richard Benjamin performed. We were competitors in the 10th U.S. Correspondence Chess Championship. It's a whole lot more fun to have him on my side. I am happy to share the credit with this fine crew, but in the end, of course, any errors that remain are my responsibility.

Permit me also to express my love and appreciation for my wife, Cheryl, and for my two sons, Aaron and Neil, who have all waited on too many occasions for Daddy to finish up his chess.

Table of Contents

chapter 3 — Rook Strategy

chapter 4 — Knight Strategy

chapter 5 — Bishop Strategy

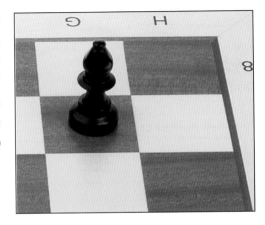

chapter 6 — Pawn Strategy

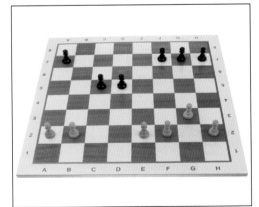

chapter 7 King and Queen Strategy

chapter 8 Opening Strategy

chapter 9 — Opening Variations

chapter 10 — Common Opening Formations

chapter 11 Middlegame Strategy

chapter 12 Elementary Checkmates

chapter 13 Attacking the King

chapter 14 Attacking Themes and Common Sacrifices

chapter **15** An Introduction to Endgames

chapter 1

An Introduction to Chess

Welcome to the game of chess. Like most games, chess has some very basic rules. Once you learn and understand those basics, you will be able to play against others, and you will be able to play through and enjoy the great matches that chess masters have played through time. In this chapter, I introduce the chessboard, how to set it up to start a game, how each piece moves, and how to begin play. I also give you the basics on chess notation, showing you the "shorthand" used in the chess world (and in this book) to indicate each move a player makes.

Chess is an ancient game of war first invented and played in China or India more than 1,000 years ago. Over time, the rules have changed, but chess remains a game of strategy and skill that continues to excite players young and old. The names of the pieces bring to mind the origins of the game—a battle. Imagine soldiers on foot with the pawns leading the charge. Imagine the cavalry on horseback; the Knights jumping into battle. Imagine the general or the King with the Queen at his side. In many battles of yore, when the King died the battle would end. And so it is in the game of chess.

Chess is played between two players who sit on opposite sides of a "chessboard." Each player takes command of a "white" or "black" army of 16 units always arranged in the same way at the start of the game. By rule, the player with the white pieces always begins the game. The players alternate moves until one player attacks the enemy King in such a way that the King cannot escape. We call that checkmate.

Many people believe that you have to be a genius to be good at chess. Being really smart helps at most things, but success in chess requires familiarity with the rules and some basic strategy, as well as practice. This book will help you to get started and to feel comfortable sitting down and playing a real game. Know that everyone starts out as a beginner.

To get the most out of this book and your chess experiences, I recommend that you buy or borrow a chessboard and a chess set to play along as you read this book. Many people have very artistic sets. Those are fine for display, but when you review the material in this book and when you play, you will want to have a standard set much like the one depicted in this book. They are not very expensive and easy to find in stores and on the Internet. If you are having trouble finding a standard set, go to the U.S. Chess Federation's website at www.uschess.org.

Chess is played on a board with 64 squares. To make it easier to view the board and move the pieces, the board has alternating light and dark squares. As you will see, it is useful to think of the board in terms of its *ranks*, *files*, and *diagonals*.

The Chessboard Setup

This chessboard is typical of those on which you will play. To set up the board correctly, place it so that a dark square is in the lower-left corner. Or, as chess players like to say, "It's white on the right."

Some boards are labeled with letters (a–h) and numbers (1–8) in the margins. Others are blank. It is perfectly fine to play with a board that does not have these letters and numbers in the margins. They are there to help you talk about the board, to name each square, and to emphasize certain features. In this book, we use a labeled board so you can easily identify the pieces and moves discussed.

For example, every board has eight *ranks* (rows) and eight *files* (columns). The 1st rank consists of the eight squares directly in front of you. The 8th rank contains the eight squares that are farthest from you. As you can see, ranks are horizontal. Try to visualize each rank in turn: the 2nd rank, the 3rd rank, and so on.

Files are vertical. The eight squares on the left side of the board are called the *a-file.* The eight squares on the right side of the board are called the *h-file.*

The alternating colors of the squares are another wonderful visual aid. For the moment, simply note that there are alternating light and dark squares and light and dark diagonals. As you will soon see, some pieces move along the ranks and files, while others move diagonally.

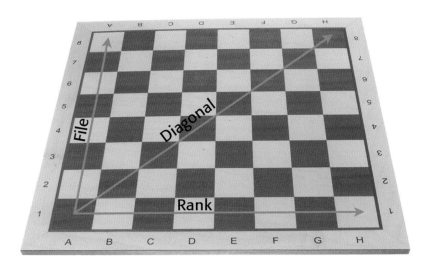

Introducing the Pieces

Your chess "team" is made up of five types of pieces: one King, one Queen, two Bishops, two Knights, and two Rooks. Each player also has eight pawns. The pieces can look different from chess set to chess set, but you will always be playing with these same chessmen.

The Five Types of Pieces

The King is truly the most important piece because you lose the game if your King is attacked and cannot escape. Kings are abbreviated with the letter K.

The Queen is considered the most powerful piece in terms of its ability to move around the board. Each player has one at the beginning of the game, though you will see, it's possible to get more! Queens are abbreviated with the letter Q.

Bishops usually have a nice, tapered appearance. At the beginning of the game, each player starts with two Bishops. They are abbreviated with the letter B.

Knights, like the cavalry, can jump into action. Each player starts with two Knights. They are abbreviated with the letter N.

Rooks are sometimes called towers or castles because they resemble the tower of a castle. Each player starts with two of them. They are abbreviated with the letter R.

CONTINUED ON NEXT PAGE

The Pawns

The pawns are the smallest unit on the chessboard. They can seem small and unimportant, but they are often very useful in helping to control territory and to launch attacks on your opponent.

Pieces and Pawns at a Glance		
Pieces and Pawns	*Abbreviation*	*How They Move*
King	K	One square in any direction, but never into a square controlled by an enemy piece.
Queen	Q	One or more squares in any direction.
Rook	R	One or more squares horizontally or vertically.
Bishop	B	One or more squares along the diagonals.
Knight	N	Like the letter L. The Knight is the only piece that can "jump" over other pieces and pawns.
Pawns	—	Forward, one square at a time. Pawns capture diagonally ahead one square. Pawns that have never moved have the option of moving forward two squares.

The chessboard setup for the start of a game is always the same. In fact, one of the great charms of chess is that you start from the same position as others have done for centuries.

Where to Place the Pieces

The Rooks begin the game in the corners. The Knights (many beginning players call them horses) are next. The Bishops start the game next to the Knights. Finally, the Queen and King fill in the remaining squares on the 1st and 8th ranks. The Queen will always start on its own color. Note that the white Queen is on a white square. The black Queen is on a dark square.

Don't forget the pawns; all eight of them are ready to start the charge. At the beginning of the game, the eight white and eight black pawns form a line just in front of the white and black pieces, across the 2nd and 7th ranks, respectively.

Note: In this book, the black side is always represented assuming a starting position at the "top" of the board on ranks 8 and 7, and white at a starting position at the "bottom" on ranks 1 and 2.

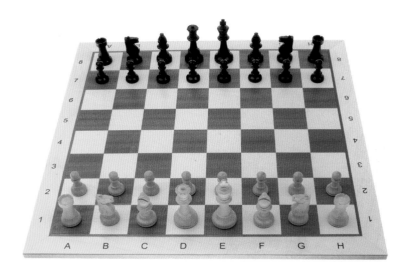

Chess is played between two players, one in control of the white pieces and one in control of the black pieces. White always has the first move.

To decide who gets white and who gets black, it is customary for one player to hide a white and black pawn in each hand. The other player then picks a hand. Whoever picks or is left with the white pawn will get the white pieces and will move first.

In the second diagram, white is advancing one of its pawns by moving it forward two squares. As you will soon see, this pawn move helps control the key squares in the very center of the chessboard and permits one of white's Bishops as well as the white Queen to move out.

How the King Moves and Captures

The King can move one square in any direction, horizontally, vertically, or diagonally. It can move forward and then back, but only one square at a time. The King can also capture any opponent's piece if it is on one of those squares. However, the King is not permitted to move into an attack. If you make a mistake and move your King into an attack, you will be required to take back your move. In other words, the King is not permitted to move so that it could then itself be captured on the next move.

How to Move the King

In this position, the white King can move legally to any of the squares highlighted in purple. A King in the center of the board can therefore move to a total of eight different squares, assuming that your opponent does not control any of those squares. By contrast, the black King in the corner can move to only three squares, those highlighted in green.

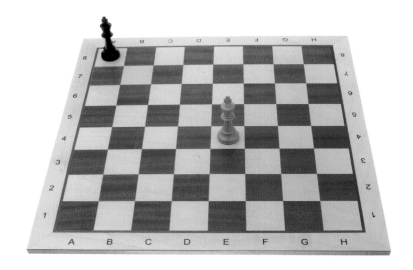

Here, only two squares are forbidden to the white King. The King cannot move to a square already occupied by its own pawn, and the King cannot move to the square marked with a red X. The white King is not permitted to move there because one of the black pawns controls that square (see page 16 to learn how the pawns move and capture).

White has several interesting options. White can capture either black pawn (to capture, white would simply remove the pawn from the board, placing the King on the square that the pawn occupied). It's fun to practice such captures. Masters have become adept at moving and snatching a piece in one fluid motion.

In this position, both Kings are facing each other. The white King can move to any of the squares highlighted in purple, and the black King can move to any of the squares highlighted in green. But neither King can move next to the other King. Simply put, a King may never move next to another King. To do so would be illegal because the other King controls those squares. It's an important point. Both Kings "control" the same three squares!

FAQ

Is a checkerboard the same as a chessboard?

It sure is! Both contain 64 alternating-color squares situated in the eight rank/eight file format. You can use a checkerboard in a pinch if you don't mind the checkerboard's traditional red squares instead of the white used for chess. In fact, you can purchase chess/checkerboard sets, which contain just one board, along with a set of checkers and a set of chessmen.

How Rooks Move and Capture

Unlike the King, a Rook can move more than one square at a time. A Rook can move any number of squares in a straight line, either horizontally or vertically, but only in one direction at a time per move. Note that a Rook cannot jump a piece of either color.

How to Move a Rook

In this position, the white Rook can move legally to any of the squares highlighted in purple. For example, it can move toward the black Knight or capture it by replacing the Knight on the square on which the Knight stood. Similarly, you might decide to capture the black Bishop, again simply by taking the Rook and placing it on the square that the Bishop occupied, being sure to remove the Bishop from the board as part of the move. A Rook is not permitted to jump either white or black pieces, so it cannot move on the other side of the white King.

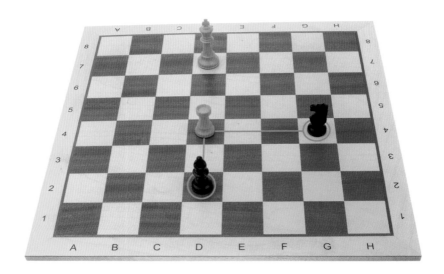

Like a Rook, a Bishop can move more than one square at a time. As opposed to a Rook, which always moves in straight lines, a Bishop can move any number of squares diagonally. A Bishop will therefore always remain on a square of the same color on which it started the game. Like a Rook, a Bishop can move forward or backward, but in only one direction at a time per move.

How to Move a Bishop

In this position, the white Bishop can move to any of the squares highlighted in purple. For example, it can move toward the black Knight or capture it. Similarly, you might decide here to capture the black Rook, again simply by replacing the black Rook with the white Bishop. The white Bishop is not permitted to jump either the white or black pieces.

How the Queen Moves and Captures

The Queen is a very powerful chess piece. It combines the powers of both a Rook and a Bishop. As such, the Queen can move horizontally, vertically, *and* diagonally. Like the King, it can move in any direction. Unlike the King, however, it can move far in one direction if there are no pieces in its path. As you might expect, the Queen cannot jump another piece.

How to Move the Queen

In this position, the white Queen can move legally to any of the squares highlighted in purple. The power of the Queen becomes obvious when you observe all of the purple squares. Clearly the Queen has many, many options. For example, the Queen can move toward or capture the black Knight. Similarly, you might decide here to capture the black Rook or the black Bishop. The Queen is not permitted to jump either the white or black pieces.

A Knight is the *only* piece that can jump over other pieces. Some players visualize the Knight moving in an L-shape—two squares horizontally and then one square vertically (or two squares vertically and then one square horizontally). More experienced players understand the move is a straight line from the starting square to the destination. As you practice your Knight moves, notice that a Knight starting on a dark square will land on a light square. And of course, a Knight starting on a light square will land on a dark square.

How to Move a Knight

In this position, the white Knight can move legally to any of the squares highlighted in purple. As you can see, it can capture the black Rook but cannot occupy the same square as the white Bishop. Remember, two pieces can never occupy the same square. Some players have some difficulty with a Knight's movement. Keep in mind that a Knight on a dark square, as in this diagram, will only be able to move to light squares. And of course, a Knight on a light square will only be able to move to dark squares.

KNIGHTS CAN JUMP

A Knight is the only chess piece permitted to jump over other pieces. In this position, the white Knight has just made the first move in the game. As you can see, it has jumped over the white pawns. Note again that the Knight, which started on a dark square, has arrived on a light square. From its new position, the Knight now has access to four new dark squares, indicated in purple.

How Pawns Move and Capture

The pawns are often called the "soul of chess." They are the only chessmen that move differently from how they capture. A pawn, like a foot soldier in war, marches ever forward, one square at a time. Unlike the other pieces, the pawn can *never* retreat. Pawns that have not yet moved have the option of making their first move two squares forward instead of just one square; but after this initial two-square move, it's one square at a time.

Pawn Dynamics

HOW TO MOVE A PAWN

In this position, the white pawn can move forward one or two squares (highlighted in purple). The white pawn has that additional two-move option because it has not yet moved. It does not matter how many moves have been played. A pawn that has never moved will have the additional option to move ahead two squares on its first move.

By contrast, the black pawn has already moved. It therefore has only one option, to advance a single square (highlighted in green).

Note: *Experienced players never refer to pawns as "pieces." Pawns are pawns. Knights, Bishops, Rooks, Queens, and Kings are considered pieces.*

HOW PAWNS CAPTURE

A pawn is the only chessman that captures differently from how it moves. It captures diagonally *only* one square ahead, as if it were fighting on its side with a short sword.

In this position, the white pawn can advance one or two squares, but it also has the opportunity to capture the black Knight. To bring about the capture, simply move the pawn diagonally one square, replacing the black Knight.

The black pawn has three options. It can advance a single square, but it can also capture either the white Knight or the white Bishop.

In order to discuss and write about chess, chess players have invented a written language that, as languages go, is the easiest language you will ever learn.

Reading and Writing Chess Moves

Just as each piece has a name, so too does every square. In each chess diagram, you will notice that there are eight letters along the top and bottom of every board (a–h) and eight numbers along each side (1–8). To identify any square, locate its letter and then its number.

For example, the square in the bottom left corner is a1. The square in the upper-right corner is h8. The square indicated is d5.

Using the names of the squares helps us to discuss the board in a very simple, clear manner. For example, in this position, the white Queen is on b1, the black Queen is on e5, and a black Bishop is on d7. White has pawns on c3 and c4. Take a moment to locate them. As you will see, it's very easy.

A numeral and period at the beginning of a notation indicates the move number. For example, in the game shown here, white's first move was pawn e2 to e4. This is notated 1.e2-e4. You will see this type of notation starting in Chapter 8, "Opening Strategy."

CONTINUED ON NEXT PAGE

Notation also permits us to talk about the movement of pieces. Remember, pieces are abbreviated as follows: K for King, Q for Queen, B for Bishop, N for Knight, and R for Rook (there isn't an abbreviation for pawn). For a refresher on these abbreviations, see "Pieces and Pawns at a Glance" on page 8. In this position, white has just moved the Queen from d1 to b1. In this book, I use the long form of the notation, "Qd1-b1," but many chess players abbreviate the move with "Qb1." As a result of white's move, the white Queen on b1 is suddenly attacking the black pawn on b6. As you can see, it's not very hard to find the black b6-pawn. To defend the b6-pawn, black might now play Re8-b8, moving the black Rook from the e8-square to b8.

Captures are simply recorded with an "x." And so in this position, if black were to move the black Queen on e5 to capture the white pawn on e4, you would write: Qe5xe4. Of course, that awful Queen move would result in losing the black Queen to the white Bishop (Bc2xe4).

When a move results in check, an attack on the enemy King, this is indicated with a "+" at the end of the notation. When a move results in checkmate, this is indicated with a "#" at the end of the move.

In this second position, white is about to promote a pawn. Promoting the e7-pawn to a Queen on e8 would be written e7-e8=Q or simply e8=Q.

Note: *If a pawn makes it all the way to the 8th rank on the other side of the board, you get to promote it to a more valuable piece, meaning you get to trade in this pawn for a Queen, Rook, Knight, or Bishop (most often players promote to a Queen because of its versatility). For more on promoting pawns, see "Promoting (and Under-Promoting) Your Pawns" in Chapter 2.*

Many beginners make the same simple mistake. After their opponent captures a piece or a pawn, they fail to recapture or "take back." A good rule of thumb is if your opponent captures one of your pieces, try to recapture a piece of equal or greater value. Generally speaking, if one side has more material than the other, they will have the advantage and will be more likely to win the game.

Protection Strategies

BE SURE TO RECAPTURE

In this example, recapturing is illustrated with pawns. Black is about to move the pawn on d5 to capture the white pawn on e4. Not to fear. As long as white is alert, black will not "win" the pawn. Rather, white can simply move the Knight to e4 (following the arrow) to recapture the pawn.

PRESERVE THE BALANCE

In this position, the situation is more complicated because more pieces have moved, but the idea of recapturing is the same. Black moves the Knight on a5 to capture the white Bishop on c4. White could respond with many moves, but white should recapture with the white pawn on d3. If white fails to recapture, black will simply move the Knight back to safety and will have taken the white Bishop without losing a thing. It may be hard to believe, but good players will almost always win the game if you give them the advantage of an extra Knight or Bishop.

Note: *If an illegal move has been played in an informal game between friends, you would simply point out the illegal move and your opponent would have another chance to move. In a tournament, that's still the case except that the opponent who touched a piece would still have to move it, albeit in a legal manner. There's also often a time penalty . . . extra time for you or less for your opponent.*

chapter

2

Special Moves

Like many other games, chess has some special moves. There are checks that attack the enemy King, checkmates that are checks from which the enemy King cannot escape, and stalemates—an end to the game in which the enemy is not in check but has no legal moves. There are discovered checks and double checks. You can transform (promote) your pawns into Queens or even under-promote your pawns to become Knights, Bishops, or Rooks. Castling permits you to move your King and Rook at the same time. And there's a special capture called *en passant* reserved just for the pawns. This chapter explains all these moves and helps you understand how you can use them to improve your play.

Whenever you attack your opponent's King, you are putting the King in check. The goal of chess is *checkmate*—to attack your opponent's King when it has no escape. You are not obliged to say "Check," and in tournaments, saying "Check" is considered rude. But who could resist saying "Checkmate"?

When the King Is Under Attack

Check simply means that a King is under attack. In this position, the black King is in check because the white Queen is attacking it along the diagonal.

On the very next move, black must make sure to stop the attack. There are three possibilities. First, the King can move out of check to any square that is not being attacked (f1, g2, h1, or h2). Note that the King cannot move to f2 because that would still be check. Simply put, the King cannot move into check.

Or black could end the attack by capturing the white Queen with the Knight (Nd5xb6).

Or black could move a piece between the attacking Queen and the King in order to interrupt the direct attack. For example, black could move the Bishop to d4 (Ba1-d4) or the Knight to e3 (Nd5-e3).

If the King is under attack and there is no immediate way to end the attack, the game is over. Note that checkmate does not actually involve removing the King from the board. In this position, the black Bishop is attacking the white King. The King has no legal moves because the other white pieces are occupying the escape squares. White cannot capture or block the attack from the Bishop. Checkmate!

Stalemates and Other Draws

Not all games end in a checkmate. Many games end in a draw, usually an agreement between the players that no one wins. This section reviews most of the types of draws. So what is a draw? That's when nobody wins. In tournaments, draws are recorded as ½ – ½, essentially half a point for each player rather than a full point for a win.

Types of Draws

A TYPICAL STALEMATE

The most exciting form of a draw is the stalemate. On a player's turn, if he or she is not in check and cannot make a legal move, this is a *stalemate*—neither side wins.

In this position, it is black's move. The black King is not in check, and it has no legal moves. It cannot capture the white pawn or move to c7 or e7 because the white King controls those squares. Similarly, the black King cannot move to c8 or e8 because the white pawn *controls* those squares. Remember that the King is not permitted to move to any square controlled by an enemy piece. This position is the most common stalemate in chess.

White appears to be well behind in this position. In fact, black is threatening to move the Rook on g3 to g1 (Rg3-g1#), checkmate. (The Knight on f3 would defend the Rook.)

However, it is white's move. White surprises black by moving the Rook on a2 to h2, check (Ra2-h2+). At first glance, the move looks terrible because black can simply capture the white Rook with the Knight. But after the Knight on f3 captures the Rook (Nf3xh2), the result is a stalemate. The white King is not in check but cannot move.

OTHER TYPES OF DRAWS

By Agreement

The most common type of draw is by agreement. At any time in a game, you can offer a draw to your opponent. Be mindful of good etiquette, however. Don't offer a draw on every move! Most chess players consider that to be rude.

Perpetual Check

In this position, white appears to have an overwhelming advantage and the prospect of a quick win, perhaps with a Rook-from-e4-to-h4 checkmate. But black on the move draws in one of two interesting ways. The most spectacular is Qb8-h2 check because, after white captures the black Queen, the result is a stalemate!

Black could also draw quickly with what is called a *perpetual check,* a never ending series of checks. Black moves the Queen from b8 to g3, check (Qb8-g3+). White cannot capture the Queen or block the attack. White therefore must move the King into the corner at h1 (Kg1-h1). To draw, black will simply check the white King on h3 (Qg3-h3+) and then again on g3 (Qh3-g3+). Reaching the same position three times in a row is an automatic draw. For a play-by-play of this draw scenario, see the next page.

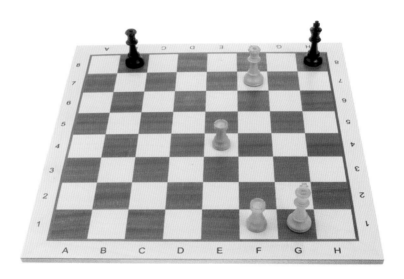

CONTINUED ON NEXT PAGE

1 White is considering a Rook move from e4 to h4, putting black in checkmate, but it's black's move.

2 Black moves its Queen from b8 to g3, check (Qb8-g3+).

3 White moves its King to h1 to get out of check (Kg1-h1).

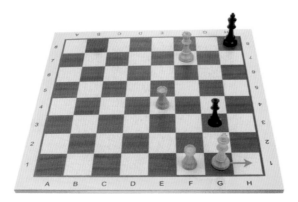

4 Black moves its Queen to check white on h3 (Qg3-h3+), and can simply move back and forth between h3 and g3, keeping the King in perpetual check.

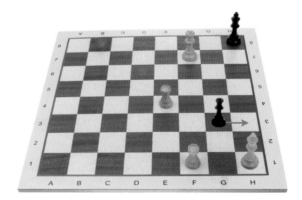

50-Move Rule

And then there's the merciful 50-move rule. If both players have made their last 50 consecutive moves without moving a pawn and without making a capture, either player can claim a draw. Obviously, you will need to have kept an accurate score sheet to make this claim! In this example from a real game, white just moved the Rook from e3 to e4 (Re3-e4) and used the 50-rule move to claim a draw. This particular game lasted a total of 170 moves.

FAQ

How much are the pieces worth?

It must be obvious by now that the Queen is much stronger than the Knight, Bishop, or Rook. After years of experience, we know the relative value of each piece. This table estimates the value of the chessmen. The basic unit, the pawn, has a value of one.

Queen	9
Rook	5
Bishop	3+
Knight	3
Pawn	1

Use the values in this table as a rough guide. A Rook is roughly worth as much as five pawns or a Knight (or Bishop) and two pawns. A Queen is worth approximately as much as a Rook, Knight, and pawn. Two Rooks are roughly equivalent to a Queen plus a pawn. Of course, in most situations, there are many other factors to consider, such the activity of the pieces and the amount of space on the board each player controls.

The King is not included in the table because, in a real sense, it has infinite value. If your opponent attacks your King and it has no escape, you lose the game. But in many positions, especially late in the game, the King can play an active role. In such situations, it might be useful to think of the King as having a value of approximately five pawns.

Note that the Bishop has a value slightly greater than the Knight. The Bishop is usually, though not always, worth a bit more than a Knight. See Chapter 5, "Bishop Strategy," for more information on why this might be so.

Discovered Checks and Double Checks

Discovered checks are among the most powerful moves in chess. The maneuver is quite simple. You move a piece, exposing an attack from a piece behind it.

If it's possible, double checks are even more exciting and deadly. Like a discovered check, a piece moves to expose a check from behind it while the piece itself also gives check. As you will see, double checks always force the King to move.

Discovered Checks

In this first position, the black King would be in check from the white Queen except that, for the moment, the white Knight on e5 is blocking the attack. With white to move, any move by the Knight will expose the attack from the Queen and place black in check, thus the discovered check. White could play the Knight to g6 check (Ne5-g6+), winning the h8-Rook on the next move. Better still, white selects the Knight to c6 check (Ne5-c6+), knowing that no matter what black does to block the check from the white Queen, the white Knight will capture the black Queen on the next move.

In this second position, black has more material than white has, but white can quickly win the black Knight and the Queen by using a discovered check. White begins by moving the Rook on b1 to b7, capturing the black b7-pawn. The Rook on b7 would place the black King in check because the Rook on b7 attacks the b8 square. The white Bishop on g2 defends the Rook on b7 (in other words, the black King cannot capture the Rook because it would then be in check from the white Bishop). Therefore, under attack from the Rook, black has no choice but to retreat the King into the corner at a8 (Kb8-a8). White then continues with a powerful discovered check: The white Rook takes the black Knight on e7 (Rb7xe7), leaving the diagonal open, with the white Bishop now holding the black King in check. After black gets out of check by moving its King back to b8 (Ka8-b8), white will move the Rook (now on e7) to capture the black Queen on f7 (Re7xf7).

See the next page for a play-by-play of this discovered check scenario.

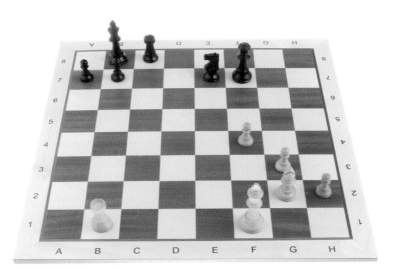

❶ The white Rook captures the black pawn on b7, putting the black King in check (Rb1-b7+).

❷ Black retreats its King to a8 (Kb8-a8).

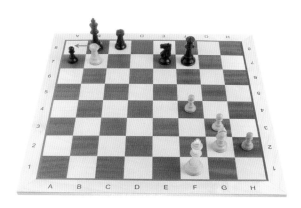

❸ The white Rook captures the black Knight on e7, revealing the discovered check from the white Bishop (Rb7xe7).

❹ Black moves its King back to b8 to get out of check (Ka8-b8). Then white moves its Rook to capture the black Queen on f7 (Re7xf7).

CONTINUED ON NEXT PAGE

Double Checks

At first glance, it appears that black has a significant advantage in this game. The Knight on f2 is attacking the white Queen and both of the white Rooks. Note also that black has two Knights while white has only one.

But white has the possibility of bringing about a powerful double check. White begins by sacrificing the Queen by moving it to d8, putting the King in check (Qd3-d8+). Black has no choice but to capture the Queen on the key d8 square (Ke8xd8).

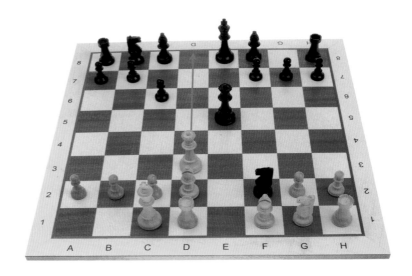

This is the position after the Queen sacrifice. White now moves the Bishop on d2 to g5 (Bd2-g5+), giving double check from both the Bishop and the Rook on d1. Note that black is attacking both of these white pieces, but it is not possible to capture both with one move.

To get out of the double check, black must move the King from d8. If the King moves to c7, white has the amazing Bishop g5 to d8 checkmate! If, instead, black moves the King from d8 to e8, white delivers checkmate by advancing the Rook to d8.

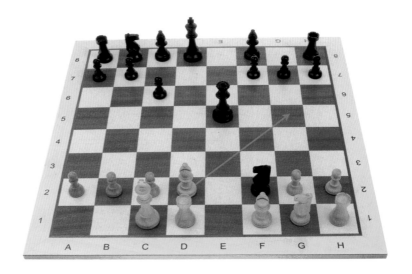

Your pawns are worth less than the King, Queen, Bishops, Knights, and Rooks, but they can help you control key squares, and they become very powerful as they approach the end of the board.

If you succeed in advancing a pawn all the way to the 8th rank, you must remove the pawn and replace it with a Queen, a Rook, a Knight, or a Bishop. Almost all the time, you will want to promote the pawn to a Queen, but there are interesting exceptions.

Promoting Your Pawns

Advance a pawn to the 8th rank and a wonderful transformation will occur. The rules require that you convert the pawn to a Knight, Bishop, Rook, or Queen. As the most powerful piece, the Queen is the most obvious choice, and most players promote to a Queen.

This position is from a game between former world chess champion Bobby Fischer (playing white) and the Russian Tigran Petrosian (playing black). Petrosian advanced the pawn on a2 to a1 (a2-a1=Q) and promoted it to a Queen. Fischer replied by advancing his h6 pawn to h7 (h6-h7). Petrosian was unable to prevent Fischer from promoting that pawn to a Queen on the next move (h7-h8=Q).

With eight pawns at the beginning of the game, you can, in theory, have a total of nine Queens on the board. It is rare, of course, to have more than two Queens. Some modern sets come with two Queens. If you have only one in your set, it is customary to use an upside-down Rook as the second Queen.

CONTINUED ON NEXT PAGE

Under-Promoting Your Pawns

Under-promotion is rare, but it's always fun when it occurs. Here, with black to move, black dares not promote the pawn on e2 to a Queen because white will quickly respond by moving its Rook on b8 to e8 (Rb8-e8+), checking the black King, and, on the next move, capturing the new Queen on e1.

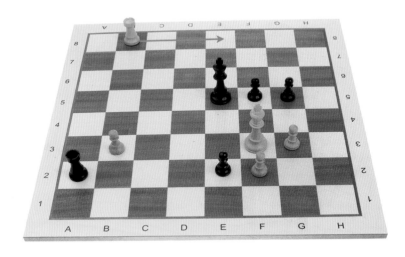

Instead, black under-promotes the e-pawn to a Knight! Suddenly, the white King is in check from the new Knight with only a single legal move: King from f3 to e3 (Kf3-e3). Note that on e3, the King no longer has any legal moves. The new Knight controls d3 and f3. The Rook on a2 controls the squares on the 2nd rank. And the black King controls d4, e4, and f4. Black should therefore attack the trapped King by advancing the f-pawn from f5 to f4 (f5-f4). That's check, with mate to follow on the next move (after two pawn captures on f4)!

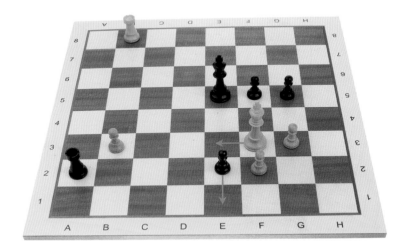

The King and the Rook can take part in a very special move, the only chess move that involves moving two pieces at the same time. This move, known as *castling*, helps bring the King to a safer square and bring the Rook toward the center.

How to Castle

Here, the white King can castle on either side of the board. To castle, follow these steps:

❶ Move the King two squares toward the Rook (in this example, from e1 to c1 or from e1 to g1.

❷ Move the Rook to the square immediately on the other side of the King (in this example, to d1 or f1).

Technically, castling is a King move, so be sure to move the King first. If you touch the Rook first in a tournament, you will be required to move just the Rook.

Here's where the King and Rook end up after castling.

CONTINUED ON NEXT PAGE

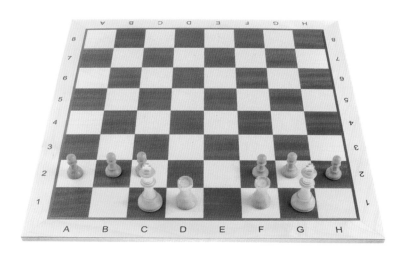

Castling
(continued)

The Rules of Castling

Note that castling is permitted only when your King and Rook have not previously moved. In addition, there are two simple rules to keep in mind:

- You cannot castle out of, through, or into check. If your King is being attacked, castling is not an option for getting out of check.

- All of the squares between the King and the Rook must be vacant.

Note that you *can* castle if your Rook is under attack. You can even castle if your Rook passes through a square controlled by your opponent.

In this diagram, white is not in check but cannot castle on the Kingside because the black Bishop on h3 controls the f1 square through which the King would have to move. White is permitted to castle Queenside despite the fact that black's Bishop on g7 is attacking the Rook on a1 and the black Queen on h7 is attacking the b1 square through which the white Rook would move.

In the early days of chess, pawns could move forward only one square at a time. When the rules changed to permit pawns to advance two squares for their first move, the French added a new rule to make sure that a pawn couldn't become a Queen without a neighboring pawn having at least one chance to capture it. Many players are not familiar with this unusual pawn capture, but it is very much a part of the game. The *en passant* (French for "while passing") capture is perhaps the trickiest chess move to learn and remember.

How to Capture En Passant

In this diagram, the white pawn on d2 has not yet moved. It has the option of moving one or two squares. If it moved ahead a single square to d3, the black pawn would clearly be able to capture it. If the white pawn moves ahead two squares, however, the black pawn on the neighboring e-file would like to have the chance to capture it before the white pawn can advance toward its *Queening square*, d8. The en passant rule applies here. For *one move only*, the black pawn can respond by capturing the white pawn as if it had moved only a single square.

Note: *From white's viewpoint, Queening squares consist of all squares in the 8th rank. For black, the Queening squares are all the squares on the 1st rank. For more on promoting pawns, see "Promoting (and Under-Promoting) Your Pawns," earlier in this chapter.*

To capture the white pawn, move the black pawn forward diagonally as if the white pawn had moved only a single square. This diagram shows the final position. Note that only pawns can capture en passant, and that only a pawn on an adjacent square can capture in this way.

EN PASSANT CAPTURE IN ACTION

In this position, it is black's move. The black King has no legal moves. In fact, black's only legal move is with the black b7-pawn. If black advances its pawn two squares from b7 to b5, white has a very strong response with the en passant capture, a5xb6. Without the en passant capture, black might actually win the game by advancing the b-pawn and promoting it to a Queen on b1. With the en passant capture, white will quickly advance the b6-pawn all the way to b8, promoting to a Queen (or Rook) with checkmate!

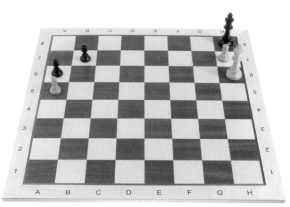

chapter 3

Rook Strategy

A Rook is a powerful piece. This chapter will help you learn how to make the most of it. Some chess players find it difficult to develop the Rooks effectively because the Rooks begin the game in the corners. Developing your pieces quickly and moving the Rooks toward the central files will help you secure control over the center of the board. And by attacking or controlling distant squares, the Rooks can help your attacks succeed. Experienced players know that Rooks belong on open files (not blocked by pawns) and that Rooks are especially effective when they get to the 7th rank to attack the enemy pawns.

To make the Rooks as good as possible, move them to open files where the pawns do not block their mobility. On open files (remember, files are the "vertical columns" on the chessboard, lettered a–h), the Rooks can move forward and help control the center and far reaches of the board.

Rooks Are Powerful on Open Files

You will often want to move a Rook to an open file where its own pawns cannot block its forward movement. In this example, the black Rook on a8 has the option of moving to any of the squares on the 8th rank. One of those squares, of course, is different. Moving the Rook from a8 to e8 (Ra8-e8) is the best move here because from e8, the Rook will help control all the squares along the 8th rank as well as the squares on the open e-file.

In the second example, there are two black Rooks and two open files. If it's good to place one Rook on an open file, it's even better to place both Rooks on open files. In this case, placing the Rooks on d8 (Ra8-d8) and e8 (Rh8-e8) will help black to control the important squares in the center of the board.

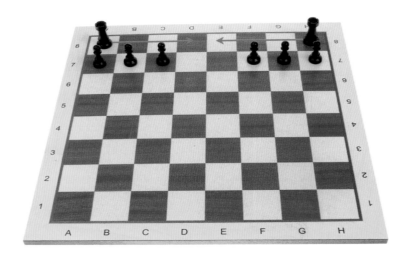

In this final example, black has both Rooks but only a single open file. You can begin by moving one of the Rooks to the e-file. Of course, that Rook will be a "good" Rook, while the other will remain "bad." To make both Rooks good, move the Rook at e8 forward, perhaps to e7 or e6. This advance will make room for the other Rook. Complete your Rook maneuver by moving the other Rook to e8. This is called "doubling Rooks" (see the next photo for the resulting doubling Rook position).

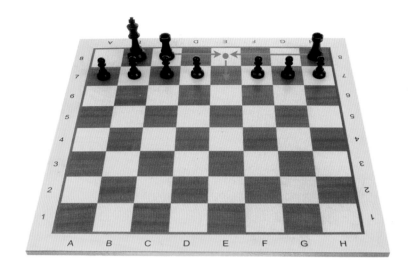

Once you control an open file with a Rook, you can often use the Rook to infiltrate your opponent's position. The Rook is especially effective when it is attacking undefended pawns deep in the enemy's position.

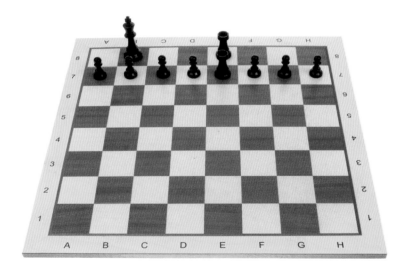

Rooks become especially powerful when they advance safely across the board to attack the enemy pawns. Don't let the term 7th rank confuse you here. When playing chess, your back row counts as rank 1, so black's 7th rank, for example, is the same as white's 2nd rank.

7th Rank Advances

In this example, the enemy pawns rest on their original squares. And so, masters often talk about advancing their Rooks to the 7th rank where the enemy pawns usually are. The key for black is to advance the Rook on e8 to e2 (Re8-e2). White will then have a problem. The black Rook on e2 will be attacking undefended white pawns on d2 and f2. White can respond by moving its Rook on b1 to d1 (Rb1-d1) or f1 (Rb1-f1), but there's clearly no way to move the Rook on b1 to defend both pawns.

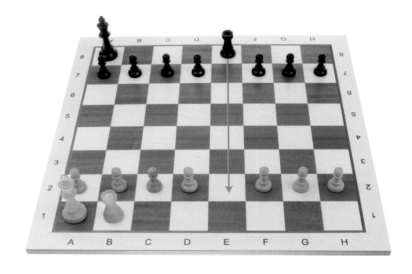

In this example, the black Rooks are dominating black's 7th rank. Black has succeeded in doubling the Rooks on the 7th rank, a catastrophe for white. On the 7th rank, the Rooks combine to place tremendous pressure on the white pawns. White has succeeded with the King on b1 and the Rook on c1 to defend the c2-pawn adequately. However, the white f2-pawn is in jeopardy. White could push the f2-pawn forward, but the black Rook on e2 would then capture the g2-pawn instead, and then go on to threaten the h2-pawn.

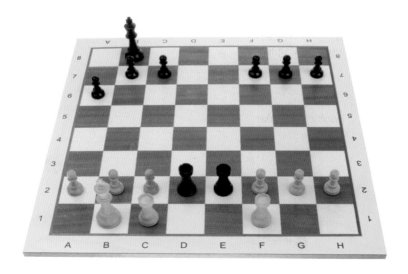

Simple Back-Rank Checkmates

Here are our first checkmates!

Rook Checkmates

One of the reasons that Rooks belong on open files is that they can often deliver checkmate all by themselves. In this example, black has an active Rook on an open file. Moreover, white has no defense along the 1st rank. Black simply moves the Rook forward all the way to e1 (Re8-e1) to attack the white King. White cannot move its King, capture the Rook on e1, or place a piece between the King and the attacking Rook. It's checkmate! Experienced players will often head off this attack by moving a pawn forward in front of their Kings; you will be surprised how often this simple attack works.

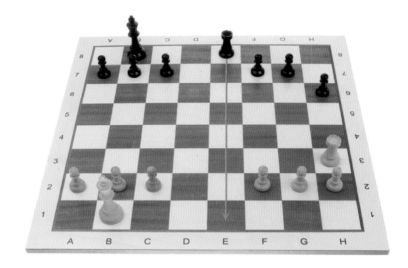

In this second example, black shows off the power of doubled Rooks. White does have a Rook defending the key e1-entry square, but black has two attacking Rooks. Black begins by advancing the Rook on e7 to e1, check (Re7-e1+). To avoid checkmate, the white Rook on g1 must capture the black Rook on e1 (Rg1xe1). White then delivers checkmate by playing Rook on e8 takes Rook on e1 (Re8xe1#).

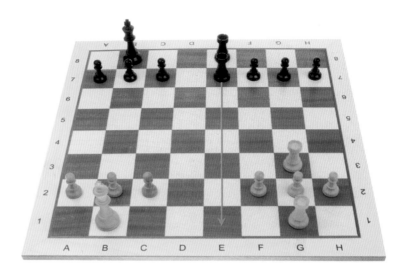

Fun with Active Rooks

As the game unfolds, the player with the most active Rooks is often the victor. Be sure to place Rooks on open files, look to advance them to undefended outposts in your opponent's position, and remain aware of the awesome power of your doubled Rooks.

Active Rooks Can Assist Mating Attacks

Here's another example of why it is so important to double your Rooks on an open file. The black Rooks are dominating the only open file on the board. As you have seen in previous examples, the Rooks will advance to the 7th rank to attack the enemy pawns. Here, however, black has a much stronger plan.

The two black Rooks combine to attack the key e1 square. White is defending the square with two Rooks. The attack will work if black can eliminate one of white's defending Rooks. Black therefore begins with the aggressive Queen sacrifice: The black Queen captures the white Rook on g1, check (Qc5xg1+). White must recapture with the Rook on h1 (Rh1xg1). The result is a simple two-on-one attack on the e1 square. Black moves its e7 Rook to e1 (Re7-e1). White then captures it with its remaining Rook (Rg1xe1). Then black advances its e8 Rook to e1 (Re8-e1#). The white King cannot escape from the final check by the e1-Rook; it's checkmate.

Rooks are also especially powerful when you place them behind *passed pawns* (pawns that are advancing toward promotion and cannot be captured by an enemy pawn). By themselves, the pawns might be successfully captured. With a Rook behind them, they become a powerful force.

Rooks and Passed Pawns

In this position, white has placed the Rook on a1 behind the passed pawn on a7. To prevent the pawn from promoting to a Queen, black was forced to play Rook to a8. The white Rook is clearly playing a strong, aggressive role. By contrast, the black Rook is quite passive and cannot move along the rank without permitting the pawn to advance. To win, white will need only to move the King from d4 to the key b7 square. On that square, the white King will attack the black Rook, forcing it to move away or be captured. If black decides to move the Rook along the 8th rank, the pawn will be able to advance and promote to Queen.

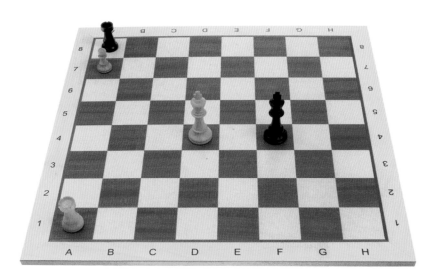

Knight Strategy

While the Bishop, Queen, and Rook can sweep across the board, the Knight is limited to its relatively short L-shaped movements. As you will see, these limited movements make it all the more important to decide early on where you can safely post the Knight and from where it can effectively assist in the battle.

Move the Knights to the Center of the Board

The experience of masters tells us that a Knight belongs in or near the center of the board, where the enemy pawns cannot attack it. From this safe post, a Knight can lash out to assist in attacks against the enemy King, to deliver unexpected forks (forks are explained in "Knight Forks Are Fun!," later in this chapter), and simply to tie down enemy movement.

Attack from the Center

In this position, the white Knight is safe from attack in the center and can move to eight different squares. From its central perch on d5, the white Knight is ready to assist in an attack on the black King or to lash out toward the black *Queenside* (the side of the board where the Queen started is called the Queenside while the side of the board on which the King started is called the Kingside). By clear contrast, the black Knight is in the corner at a8, where it will likely have very little effect on what will happen next.

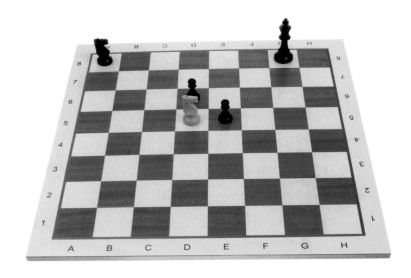

In this position, the white Knight controls eight squares because it is actively placed in the middle of the board. Note that the Knight is occupying a light square on e4 and, as a result, is attacking eight different dark squares.

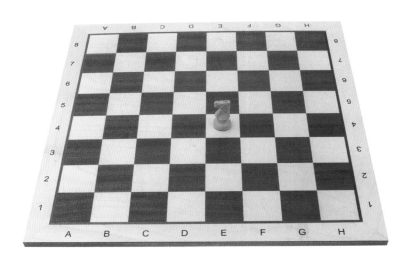

If you move or place a Knight on a dark square, for example on d4, it would be attacking eight different light squares. Observing the light square/dark square relationship here can help you become more comfortable with the movement of the Knight.

By contrast, if you place the Knight on the side of the board, the Knight will have access to only four squares. In this case, the Knight on d8 can move only to b7, c6, e6, and f7. That's why we say that "a Knight on the rim is grim."

In this position, the white Knight on the a2 square has access to only three squares: b4, c3, and c1. The black Knight in the corner on h8 can move only to two light squares: f7 and g6. There's a rhyme for that too: "A Knight in the corner makes you a mourner."

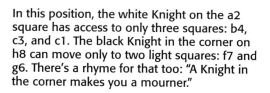
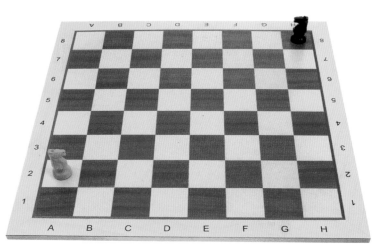

Place Your Knights Where the Enemy Pawns Can't Attack Them

The actual rule for Knight strategy is a bit more complicated than simply moving your Knights to the center of the board. The key is to move your Knights to central squares that your opponent's pawns cannot attack.

Avoid Pawn Attacks

Black has just responded to white's opening move of pawn from e2 to e4 (e2-e4) with Knight g8 to f6 (Ng8-f6). At first, black's move seems strong because the Knight has developed quickly toward the center and is attacking the white pawn on e4. However, on white's second move, the pawn on e4 can advance again to e5 (e4-e5), attacking the black Knight on f6. The black Knight would need to move again to avoid its loss, but moving the Knight to e4 would invite another pawn attack d2 to d3 (d2-d3). Moving the black Knight to d5 (Nf6-d5), a better move, would nonetheless invite white to attack the Knight with c2 to c4 (c2-c4). As you can see from this example, advancing your Knights to the center of the board isn't enough; read on.

In this example , the white Knight is on its starting g1-square. The advance of black's central pawns has created a "hole" in black's pawn structure on the d5 square. Note that the black pawns will not be able to attack or capture the white Knight if it's on d5, and from the d5 hole, the Knight would help to control eight squares. On d5, the Knight would be able to assist a Kingside attack or possibly deliver forks on the c7 square (imagine a black Rook on a8 and the black King on e8). To learn about forks, see "Knight Forks Are Fun!," on the next page. The arrows show the fastest and safest path for the Knight to follow to reach the key d5 square in this scenario: g1-e2-c3-d5.

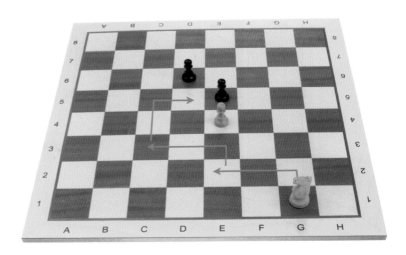

Knight Forks Are Fun!

The Knight can attack two or more pieces at the same time. When a Knight attacks two pieces at once, we call it a *Knight fork*. An attack on more than two pieces is called a *family fork*. In practice, it is rare for a Knight to attack more than two pieces at a time, but forks are often the culmination of complex maneuvers and tactical intrigue.

Family Fork

Here's a position from a sample game, with black set to move. As you can see, the white Knight on d5 is attacking the black Queen on e7. If the black Queen moves forward one square from e7 to e6, do you see how white can move the white Knight to deliver a family fork?

The answer is Knight from d5 to c7 (Nd5-c7); resulting in check, as well as a family fork. The white Knight on c7 is attacking black's Knight (Ke8), Queen (Qe6), Rook (Ra8), as well as the Bishop (Ba6).

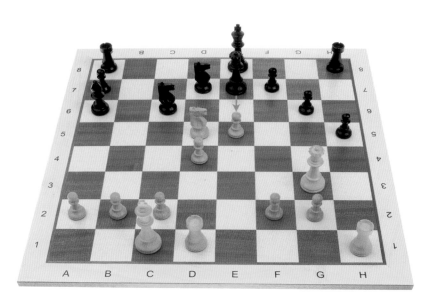

CONTINUED ON NEXT PAGE

In this more difficult example, white combines a wonderful Queen sacrifice with a clever Knight fork to gain a decisive material advantage. Note that the white Knight on d5 is powerfully located in the center, even though it is being attacked by a black pawn on e6.

As chess books like to say, it's white to move and win, in this case by winning a piece. White begins by moving its Knight to f6, putting the King in check (Nd5-f6+). Note that black cannot capture the Knight with its Bishop because the white Queen on g4 is *pinning* the Bishop on g7. Simply put, you are not allowed to make a move that places your King in check. Black must therefore respond by moving the King to f7 or into the corner to h8. White then has a wonderful combination ending with a Knight fork. White captures the black Bishop with its Queen, putting the King in check (Qg4xg7+). Black must respond by recapturing the Queen with its King (Kxg7). This then yields a Knight fork opportunity for white that will regain the Black Queen. Can you find the solution?

The answer is Knight to e8, check (Nf6-e8+), forking the King and Queen. The play-by-play of this combination is detailed on the next page.

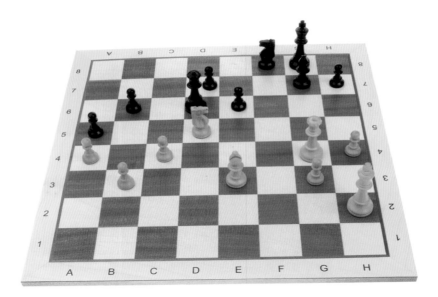

1 White moves Knight to f6, putting the King in check (Nd5-f6+).

2 Black's King moves to f7 to get out of check (Kg8-f7) (the King could also move to h8).

3 White's Queen captures the black Bishop, putting the King in check again (Qg4xg7+).

4 Black responds, capturing white's Queen with the King (Kxg7). This reveals the Knight fork opportunity for white (Nf6-e8+), forking the King and Queen.

chapter

Bishop Strategy

The Bishop is forever committed to traveling on the same color. To make sure that the Bishop will have the most substantial effect on the position, it is important not to fix your pawns on the color of your Bishop. In an open board where the pawns are mobile, the Bishop can be a very powerful piece. You will soon see pins, skewers, and Bishops that can dominate Knights and even Rooks. However, in a closed position where many of the pawns are fixed, the Bishop's mobility can be seriously limited.

Bad Bishops and Good Bishops

Just as there are good Rooks (on open files) and good Knights (in the center where the enemy pawns can't attack them), there are good Bishops and bad Bishops. From experience, it is clear that Bishops are good as long as you don't limit their mobility behind pawns that are fixed (set on the same color as the Bishop).

A VERY BAD BISHOP

In this situation, the white Bishop on f1 can safely move around to g2, h3, and even h1. You can immediately see that, while the Bishop remains on the board, it will have no meaningful effect on the rest of the game. In a real sense, white's pawns on e2, f3, and g4 have imprisoned or trapped their own light-squared Bishop. The simplest advice: Don't let this happen to you!

GOOD VS. BAD

Most of the time, Bishops are not quite that bad, but the principle remains important. Do not fix pawns on the same color as your Bishop. In this example, the two pawns are considered *fixed* because they cannot advance. The Bishop on b2 is considered "bad" because the white pawn on d4 is fixed on its color. By contrast, the black Bishop on g7 is considered "good" because it is attacking a fixed white pawn.

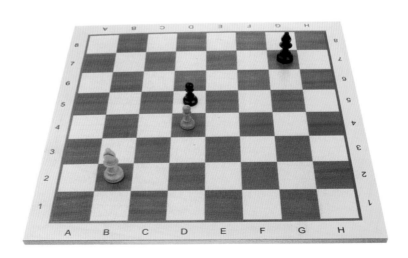

Bishops Can Dominate Knights

One reason that Bishops are worth slightly more than Knights is that the Bishop can dominate a Knight on the open board.

In this position, the white Bishop on e5 controls all four of the squares to which the black Knight on h5 can move.

To improve your play, you should play against others and also play through the games of some the world's greatest players. As you play through master games, time and again, you will observe the same pattern: Bishops three squares away from enemy Knights, dominating them just as they do in this example.

Fianchettos

Fianchetto is Italian for "on the flank." In chess, a fianchetto is a special formation of pawns that give the Bishop an opportunity to take control over the longest diagonal on the chessboard. White can fianchetto the Bishop on the Queenside by playing b2-b3 and then Bc1-b2. On the Kingside, white can play g2-g3 and then Bf1-g2. Many players enjoy these formations because fianchettoed Bishops have such sweeping control through the board.

The Formation

At the beginning of a game, you have an opportunity to place your Bishop quickly on the board's longest diagonal, setting up a fianchetto. In this position, after advancing the g-pawn to g3 (g2-g3), white can play Bishop f1 to g2 (Bf1-g2). Many players like this maneuver, but white must be careful when advancing the g-pawn that black is not able to capture the white Rook on h1 with a Bishop or a Queen coming straight down the long diagonal.

Here, all of the Bishops have been fianchettoed (flanked by their pawns). Note that both sides have been very careful, developing the Knights to f3 and f6 to prevent any of the Bishops from capturing another Bishop.

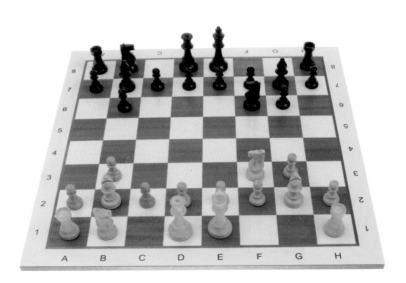

Bishops of Opposite Color

Light-squared Bishops and dark-squared Bishops can never capture one another. That simple fact usually means that games ending with opposite-colored Bishops result in draws.

Opposite-Colored Bishops Often Result in a Draw

In this position, black appears to have a significant two-pawn advantage. However, white has a light-squared Bishop, while black's Bishop can travel only on the dark squares. The two can never come into direct conflict. White can effectively blockade the black pawns by moving its Bishop to light squares that stay in contact with the d3 square. For example, white could simply shuttle the Bishop back and forth between d3 and c2. If black moved the King around to c3 in order to prevent Bishop to c2, the white Bishop could move instead to e4. Simply put, there's no safe way for black to advance the pawns.

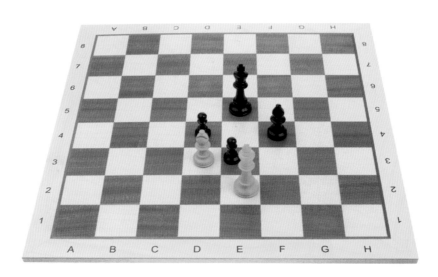

Skewers are dramatic attacks by the Bishop, usually involving a check, that often net a Rook or a Queen. *Pins* are much more common maneuvers. A pin begins with a Bishop attacking a piece, usually a Knight. In some cases, a movement by the Knight would expose the Queen to attack. In other cases, the Knight cannot move, because the Bishop would then be attacking the King. The Knight is thus, pinned by the Bishop.

SKEWERS

In this position, it is white's move. White can carry out a skewer in two different ways. First, white could attack or check the black King by playing Bishop on d1 to f3 (Bd1-f3). The black King on d5 would have to move, permitting white to capture the Rook on a8 (Bf3xa8). Better still, white could play Bishop to b3, check (Bd1-b3+). Here, the skewer will net the Queen on g8 (Bb3xg8).

PINS

In this position, there are two pins. Note that the white Bishop on b5 is pinning the black Knight on c6 to the black King. This is called an *absolute pin* because the Knight on c6 cannot legally move (remember, you cannot make a move that results in putting your King in check).

By contrast, the black Bishop on g4 is pinning the white Knight on f3 to the white Queen. This is called a *relative pin* because the Knight on f3 is permitted to move. Such moves are often unwise though, because moving the Knight would result in the loss of the white Queen.

It is far more common, in master play, for players to "unpin" with a move like Bishop f1 to e2 (Bf1-e2), as seen in the photo at the top of this page. Or, white could simply challenge the black Bishop by moving the pawn from h2 to h3 (h2-h3); masters call such pawn maneuvers "putting the question to" or "kicking" the Bishop.

While Bishops are often better than Knights, there are exceptions to the rule. A good Knight (in the center of the board where the enemy pawns cannot attack it) is almost always better than a bad Bishop (locked in by its own pawns).

In this example, material is even—black and white are evenly matched in the number and value of their pieces. However, black's Knight is wonderfully posted, while the white Bishop has little scope. In this position, it is white's turn to move, but every move that white can make will result in a winning advantage for black. If, for example, white moves the Bishop, black will be able to capture it with its Knight and then infiltrate with the King.

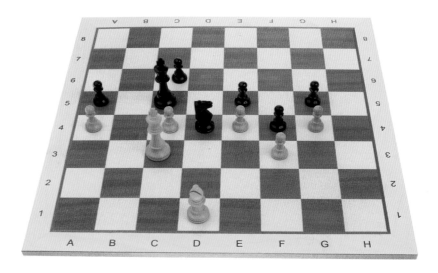

Bishops Can Dominate Rooks

In almost all situations, Rooks are stronger than Bishops. Perhaps you will be fortunate to skewer a Rook or to pin a Rook to a Queen or a King.

There is another way for a Bishop to dominate a Rook. It simply requires some help, in this case from an advanced pawn.

In this example, both Bishops are dominating a Rook. The white Bishop on f8, for example, has trapped the black Rook on g8 with help from the pawn on g7. If the Rook moves to h8, the pawn will capture it. If the Rook captures the Bishop on f8, the pawn will then capture it. If the Rook captures the pawn on g7, the Bf8 will capture it.

Similarly, the black Bishop on b2, with help from the advanced black a-pawn, has trapped the white Rook. If the Rook moves to a1 or captures the a3-pawn, the Bishop can capture it. And if the Rook on a2 captures the Bishop on b2, the a3-pawn will be able to recapture. Imagine trapping a Rook in this way and then bringing up another pawn or piece to attack it.

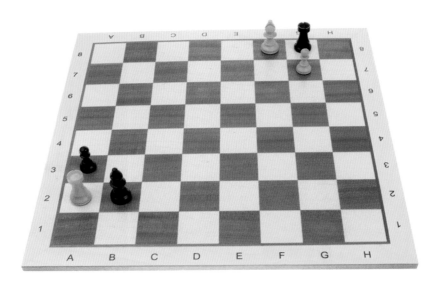

This position was reached in the famous 1972 World Championship match between Bobby Fischer and the Russian Boris Spassky. Spassky, playing white, had just played Bishop to e7 and was threatening to play Bishop e7 to f8 (Be7-f8) and then pawn g7 to g8 (g7-g8) to promote to Queen (g7-g8=Q)! Fischer had no choice but to prevent that threat with Rook a8 to g8 (Ra8-g8). Naturally, Spassky followed up with Bishop e7 to f8 (Be7-f8), trapping Fischer's Rook. In spite of having his Rook trapped, Fischer nonetheless went on to win the game and the match.

FACT

U.S.-born Bobby Fischer is viewed by many chess players as the greatest chess player in history. He took the chess world by storm in 1972, when he challenged and defeated reigning World Champion, Russian Boris Spassky. This meeting was coined as the "Match of the Century." Fischer's convincing victory over Spassky brought chess into the international limelight and elevated Fischer to celebrity status. Fischer's win was viewed by many as a symbolic Western victory during the Cold War.

chapter 6

Pawn Strategy

Unlike Kings, Queens, Bishops, Knights, and Rooks, pawns can move in only one direction: forward, ever forward. Reach the final rank and the lowly pawn, the foot soldier of chess, can transform itself into any piece except a King (players most often opt to promote to a Queen). But there is much more to pawns than just the quest to promote into a more powerful piece. As the pawns move forward, they open up diagonals for the Bishops, protect other pieces, and often lead the way for attacks. They can pry open an opponent's Kingside, but they can also spell doom when they become weak, and are then subject to capture.

Don't Double Your Pawns

When pawns are one in front of the other, we refer to them as *doubled pawns*. Doubled pawns occur when a pawn captures and moves in front of another pawn. There are exceptions to most rules in chess, but you should usually try to recapture with a piece rather than with a pawn to avoid the weakness of doubled pawns.

The Weaknesses of Doubled (and Tripled) Pawns

In this position, white has doubled pawns on the f-file, while black has tripled pawns on the c-file. These pawns are weak because they cannot defend one another. If you were playing white, for example, you might attack the black pawns with Rooks along the c-file, and perhaps also with your other pieces. Black might decide to try to defend the pawns or, alternatively, attack the weak white doubled pawns.

Here, black has not one but two sets of doubled pawns. White's strategy is clear. White has doubled the white Rooks on the c-file and will, on the next move, capture the weak black pawn on c6. In contrast, the white pawn structure seems quite strong with no obvious weaknesses. As a result, black cannot easily mount a counterattack on white's position.

It is worth noting that there are many situations in which you need not be in rush to attack such weaknesses. By all means do so if you see a clear win as a result, as in this situation, but keep in mind that weaknesses such as doubled pawns are "structural" in that the weaknesses will usually be there for the whole game, and you will easily be able to capture such pawns once all of your pieces are well developed.

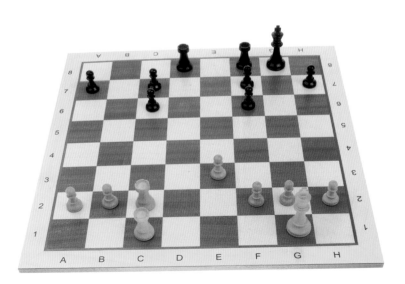

Pawns are generally more secure and harder to attack when they are connected and able to defend one another. By contrast, when the pawns are scattered around the board, they are easier to attack.

The Fewer Pawn Islands the Better

Here, white has two *pawn islands*. Pawn islands consist of a single pawn or group of side-by-side pawns that are separated from other pawns by open files. The white pawns on the a-, b-, and c-files form one island, while the white pawns on the f-, g-, and h-files form the other island. Side-by-side, these pawns do not defend one another, but we consider these strong formations because, unlike the doubled pawns we just saw, they contain no permanent weaknesses and are capable of defending one another.

By contrast, the black pawns in this diagram form a total of four pawn islands and are considered much weaker. Three of the pawns have no neighbors. Therefore, if attacked, these pawns would need to be defended by Knights, Bishops, Rooks, or Queens, pieces that in most cases have more important roles to play than to defend a lowly pawn.

The general rule here is simple: During the game, try to have fewer pawn islands than your opponent.

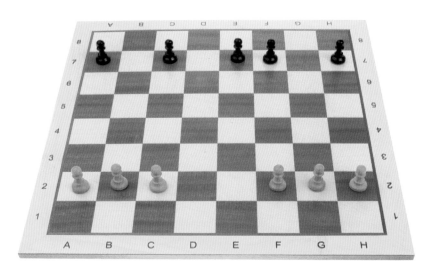

Some Doubled Pawns Are Strong

Many beginning players become so fearful of doubling their pawns that they miss situations when doubled pawns can be strong.

Double Pawns Supporting the Center

In the following position, the black Knight has just captured on the e3 square. White could automatically recapture with the Queen to avoid doubling the white pawns on the e-file. A great American chess player, Frank Marshall, reached this position in a game against Abraham Kupchik in 1915. Marshall decided that capturing with the pawn had some advantages that outweighed the structural weakness of doubling the pawns.

Here is the position after the pawn capture. The new pawn on e3 helps to support the white center by defending the white d4-pawn. More important, by recapturing with the pawn, white has opened up the f-file for the Rook. To be sure, white now has four pawn islands while black has only two, but Marshall, who went on to win the game, felt that having both the Queen and the Rook on the open file and the strengthened center more than compensated for the doubled pawns and the extra pawn island.

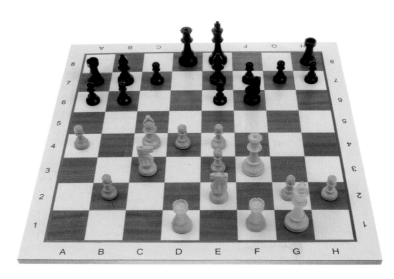

In many openings, the pawns form *chains* along a diagonal. Compare these chains to birds flying in formation. When three birds fly overhead in formation, the best strategy for a hunter is to aim for the last bird. The other birds may hear the shot, but they won't actually see that the bird has been hit. Similarly, the pawn at the rear of the chain is the weakest because no other pawn defends it. The best strategy is to aim your attack at the rear of your opponent's pawn chain.

Introducing Pawn Chains

In this position, the three white pawns are forming a chain. Note that two of the three white pawns are defended. The most advanced white pawn on e5 is defended by the pawn on d4. The pawn on d4 is defended by the pawn on c3. By contrast, the white pawn on c3 is completely undefended. The pawn in the rear of the chain is considered the weakest of the pawns precisely because the other pawns can no longer protect it.

The weak pawn in the chain often becomes the main target of the attack by your opponent. In this position, black has prepared and will now play the move c7 to c5 (c7-c5).

If white should capture black's c5-pawn (d4xc5), both of white's remaining pawns would be weak and subject to capture. White would try a similar strategy by advancing the f-pawn from f2 to f4 (f2-f4). White's plan would then be to play f4 to f5 (f4-f5) with the idea of attacking the weak e6-pawn in black's short pawn chain.

Note: *For more on attacking pawn chains, see "Backward Pawns" later in this chapter.*

CONTINUED ON NEXT PAGE

Pawn Chains
(continued)

This position offers a more practical example. White, on the attack, advances the pawn to e6 (e5-e6) where it attacks the base of black's f7-g6-h5 pawn chain. If black responds by capturing white's e6-pawn (f7xe6), white will be able to respond with Queen to g6 to capture the middle pawn in the chain, simultaneously putting the King in check (Q3-g6+).

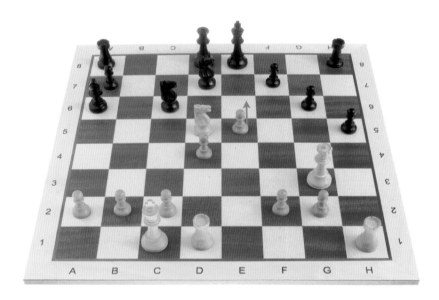

TIP

Want to learn more about pawns and other chess strategies? Join a local chess club. Most chess clubs have players from beginners through master. You can use the United States Chess Federation's website (www.uschess.org/directories/AffiliateSearch/) to look for clubs in your area. All chess clubs welcome new and intermediate players, and most offer free lectures and lessons.

Apart from meeting new people, a chess club is a great place simply to play and improve. If there isn't an existing chess club in your area, gather some other interested players and start one. The U.S. Chess Federation makes starting a new club easy. For more on becoming an affiliate, visit their website.

One key goal for the pawns, of course, is to promote at least one to a Queen by advancing it to the end of the board. Sometimes, pawns are able to advance without any opposition. More often, you will have to find a way to push your pawns successfully past your opponent's pawns. A *pawn majority* means that one player has more pawns than the opponent on one side of the board. As you will see, some pawn majorities are more useful than others.

USEFUL PAWN MAJORITIES

In this position, both sides have useful pawn majorities. On the Queenside, for example, white has three advanced pawns facing only two black pawns. With white to move, white can make significant progress toward promoting a pawn by advancing the c-pawn forward (c5-c6). With no black pawn on c7, white threatens simply to advance the c-pawn from c6 to c7. Black can delay the advance of the white pawn temporarily by capturing on c6 (b7xc6), but white will be able to use the power of this majority to force a white pawn through no matter what black tries.

Black, of course, has a useful pawn majority on the Kingside. Knowing that it is not possible to prevent white from Queening a pawn, black might instead seek a Queen by advancing the h-pawn forward to h3 (h4-h3). Here too, white can delay the advance with a capture (g2xh3), but the majority will succeed in making a passed pawn (remember, "passed pawn" is just another term for a pawn that can't be opposed by an enemy pawn).

NOT USEFUL PAWN MAJORITIES

In this next position, on the Queenside, white has a three-pawn majority against only two for black, but the pawns are all fixed and the extra pawn is not capable of being forced through for promotion.

Similarly, on the Kingside, black has a pawn majority, but the pawn majority is not useful. Any effort by black to advance the g-pawn will result in the pawn's capture and in a dangerous passed pawn for white.

Isolated Pawns

Simply put, *isolated pawns* are single pawn islands that have no pawns on either side. Such pawns therefore cannot be defended by a pawn. Even without help, such pawns can advance aggressively, but all too often, isolated pawns are blocked, attacked, and captured.

HOW TO SPOT AN ISOLATED PAWN

In this position, white and black both have three pawn islands. Black's smallest island, the e6-pawn, is an isolated pawn. Notice there are no black pawns on the d-file or on the f-file. If a white piece was to attack the black e6-pawn, black would have to defend the isolated e-pawn with a piece because there are no pawns to do the job. To try to eliminate the isolated pawn, black might try to push it to e5 in an effort to exchange it.

Similarly, one of white's island is the isolated pawn on d4. Faced with a lasting weakness, white might consider advancing the pawn to d5 in an effort to exchange it for black's e6-pawn. Isolated pawns like these play an important role in shaping strategy. Here, black might try to double Rooks. For example, black might place a Rook or two on the d-file to place pressure on or perhaps capture the isolated white d-pawn. White could try a similar strategy, doubling the white Rooks on the e-file to attack black's weak e6-pawn.

BLOCKADE ISOLATED PAWNS WITH YOUR KNIGHTS

In this next position, white and black have both succeeded in blockading each other's isolated pawns. The white Knight on e5 occupies a key square, right in the center of the board where the black pawns will not be able to attack it.

Similarly, the black Knight on d5 blockades white's isolated d-pawn. From these key squares, the Knights will often have opportunities to lash out with forks or to assist in the attacks on each other's Kings.

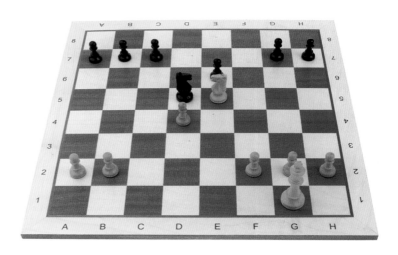

The pawn in the rear of a pawn chain is called a *backward pawn*. There are many situations in which backward pawns are very weak and especially open to attack.

HOW TO SPOT A BACKWARD PAWN

There are several backward pawns in the following position. Black's a7-pawn is a glaring example. If black moves the a7-pawn forward, white will be able to capture it on a6. Note that white would be able to capture en passant if black advanced the a-pawn two squares to a5. For a refresher on en passant captures, see Chapter 2, "Special Moves."

There are three other backward pawns in this position: f5, f2, and h2. Imagine blockading these pawns with a Knight, or mounting an attack on them with your Bishops, Rooks, and Queen.

ATTACKING A BACKWARD PAWN

In this position, white has succeeded in fixing and attacking black's backward a7-pawn with both Rooks. Because no pawns can defend the backward pawn, black will either have to defend the pawn with a piece or else let white capture it. Try to imagine how to defend the a7-pawn. Perhaps you would move a Bishop to b8. Or perhaps, you would use two Rooks along the 7th rank.

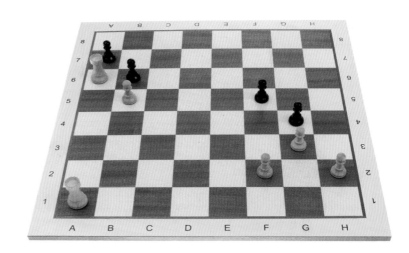

Hanging Pawns

Pawn islands that have two pawns side by side are often called *hanging pawns*. Hanging pawns are sometimes weak and sometimes strong. If you are on the attack, try to get your opponent to move one of the pawns and then blockade the pawn chain that emerges.

HOW TO SPOT HANGING PAWNS

In this position, black's pawns on c5 and d5 are said to be "hanging." The word suggests danger, and as you will see, such pawns can bring about wonderful attacking chances or be the cause of defeat. With white to play, imagine how you might organize your pieces to attack either the c5- or the d5-pawn. Perhaps you might double your Rooks on the c- or d-file. Perhaps you might use your Knights to attack one of the pawns. In this section, there are several examples that will illustrate the potential strength and weakness of hanging pawns.

HANGING PAWNS CAN BE STRONG

In this position, the hanging pawns have helped black to attack the white pawn on e2 (d5-d4). Notice that the advanced black pawn on d4 helps to control the key e3 square. White cannot advance the e2-pawn without black having an opportunity to capture with the d-pawn on e3. Notice that black has assembled a massive amount of pressure on the white e2-pawn. The two Rooks and the black Bishop on a6 are all combining to pressure white's e2-pawn. It should be clear that black's hanging pawns are assisting in the attack. The most meaningful weakness in the position is on e2.

Similarly, in this position, the hanging pawns have helped black to attack the white pawn on b2. In this case, black has advanced the c-pawn to c4 (c5-c4), helping to fix and attack the key white pawn on b2. Black's pieces are poised here for the attack, with both Rooks and the black Bishop joining in the attack on the b2-pawn. In this case, the most meaningful pawn weakness is on b2.

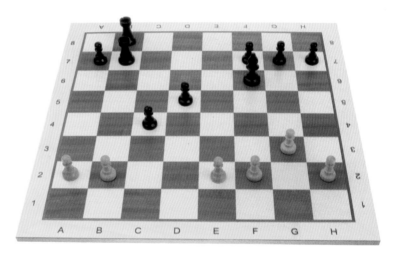

CONTINUED ON NEXT PAGE

HANGING PAWNS CAN BE WEAK

In this position, the hanging pawns are very weak. Black has advanced the d-pawn to d4 (d5-d4), creating a "hole" in the pawn structure on c4. Rather than play passively and permit an attack on the e2-pawn, white has responded aggressively by fixing and then attacking the backward pawn on c5. As you can see, all four of the white pieces have joined in on the attack on black's c5-pawn.

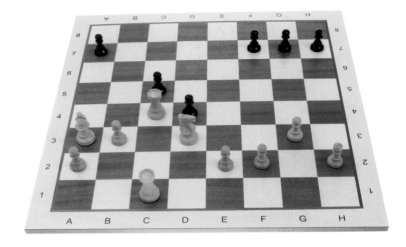

Here, the hanging pawns are also very weak. This time, black has pushed the c-pawn to c4 (c5-c4), leaving a backward pawn on d5. White has again responded aggressively by mounting a huge attack on the backward d5-pawn. As you can see, the white Knight, the two white Rooks, and white's light-squared Bishop have all joined in the attack.

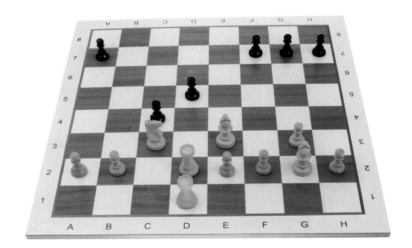

Pawn Masses

Obviously, pawns can become more and more powerful as they advance toward the end of the board. By themselves, however, they can be vulnerable, blocked, and then captured.

Instead, imagine a group or *mass* of pawns advancing in tandem. Such pawn masses are especially strong and can overwhelm your opponent's position.

A Powerful Pawn Mass

In this position, three black pawns have crashed through the enemy lines and together, threaten to overwhelm the white army. The simplest way for black to proceed is to advance the black d-pawn forward from d4 to d3 (d4-d3). On d3, the well-protected pawn attacks the white Bishop on e2. Note that the Bishop, once attacked, would have no safe retreats.

As you might imagine, pawn masses are fun to have. Make sure, of course, that you protect your pawns carefully. For example, in this position, if it were white's move, the white Bishop could capture the undefended black c4-pawn or the white Queen could safely capture the d4-pawn.

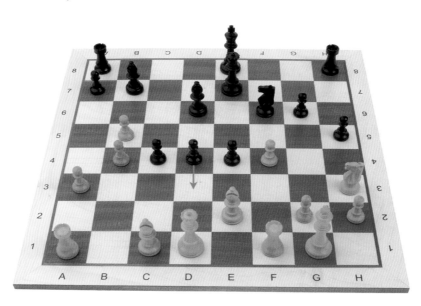

The lowly pawn will occasionally have a chance to show off some power. Look for opportunities to attack two pieces at the same time with your pawns. These pawn forks will almost always result in a significant gain of material, the capture of a piece worth much more than a single pawn.

Pawn Forks

Here's a simple example. By advancing the white e-pawn to e5, the little white pawn will be attacking the black Rook and Knight at the same time. Be on the lookout for such moves because they often result in the gain of material.

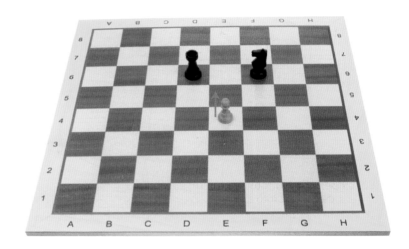

A REAL LIFE EXAMPLE

In this position, white has just moved the dark-squared Bishop to f4. By advancing the black e-pawn from e6 to e5 (e6-e5), black can fork the white Bishop and the white Knight on d4.

If white responds by moving the Knight, black could capture the Bishop. And of course, if white were to retreat the Bishop, black could capture the Knight.

How do you stop a passed pawn? Placing a Queen or a Rook in the path of a passed pawn may not be the solution because it's too easy to force such a valuable piece to move. To prevent your opponent's passed pawn from advancing, try blockading it with a Knight.

In the position at the right, the white h2-pawn is the only passed pawn because it can proceed down the h-file, all the way to the h8 Queening square without any black pawn ever being able to capture it.

Stopping Passed Pawns

In this position, with black to move, the Knight can prevent the white a-pawn from promoting into a Queen by blockading the pawn. Move the Knight into the corner at a8, and you will prevent the further advance of the a-pawn.

Knights usually make the best blockaders. If you block a passed pawn with a more powerful piece, a Queen for example, the Queen would have to move off its blockading square if attacked by a piece of lesser value. The Knight makes the best blockader because it is the least valuable among the major (Queen and Rook) and minor (Bishop and Knight) pieces.

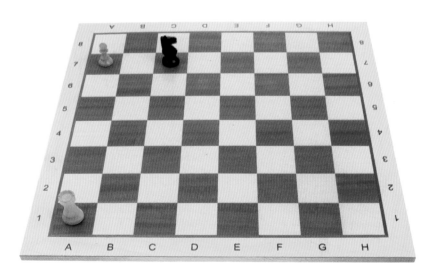

Every Pawn Move Creates a Weakness

As you have seen, pawn moves can be very strong. Pawns can fork, and they can promote into Queens. However, every pawn move also creates a weakness. As pawns move forward, they give up control over squares that can often become important bases for the opponent's pieces. Always consider whether your advance of a pawn is more important than the weakness that you will create.

The Advance of a Pawn Creates a Weakness

In this position, with black to move, black is considering the possibility of advancing the pawn on e6 to e5. The pawn move makes some sense. The pawn will move forward and force the white Knight on d4 to move. However, the pawn on e6 currently defends the d5 and f5 squares. If black advances the e-pawn to e5, both the d5 and f5 squares will become weak.

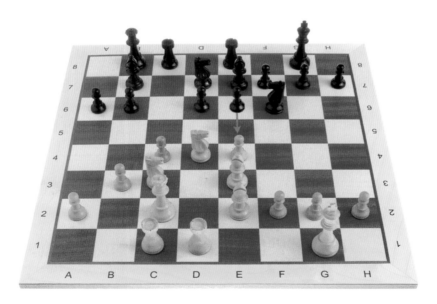

Here is the position after the advance of the black e-pawn. It is true that the white Knight on d4 must move, but white has the strong move Knight d4 to f5 (Nd4-f5). On f5, the white Knight attacks the black Bishop on e7 and places more pressure on what is now a backward black pawn on d6.

More important, perhaps, the advance of the black e-pawn has created a hole in the black pawn structure on the key central d5-square. For example, white is likely, within a few moves, to move the Knight on c3 into the hole on d5. Both of these key moves, Knight to f5 (Nd4-f5) and Knight to d5 (Nc3-d5), are possible because black decided to advance the e-pawn to e5. So keep in mind, all pawn moves create such weaknesses. Be sure to locate the weaknesses and consider their importance before you lash out with pawn moves.

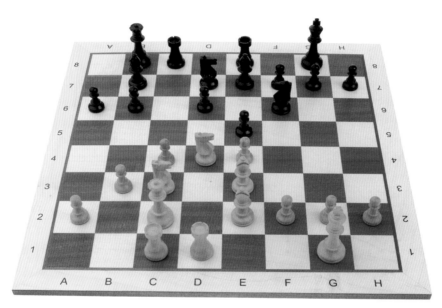

King and Queen Strategy

The King and Queen are the two strongest pieces. The Queen has tremendous scope, especially in the open board, but it is important not to bring the Queen out too early. If you do, you might find that your opponent is able to attack the Queen and make it move again and again, often a clear waste of time.

The King, of course, is the most important piece. If it is attacked and has no escape, you lose the game. Therefore, you typically want to safeguard your King before you begin your attacks. In most games, you will usually want to castle to safeguard your King and activate a Rook. Once castled, try not to move the pawns in front of your King. As you saw in Chapter 6, every pawn move creates weaknesses that your opponent may be able to exploit.

Don't Develop Your Queen Early

Most of the time, you will want to develop your Knights, Bishops, and perhaps also your Rooks before you bring out your Queen. The Queen is so valuable that it is difficult early on to be sure exactly where the Queen belongs. If you advance your Queen into the middle of the board, your opponent will have a chance, for example, to develop their Knights, Bishops, and Rooks and, at the same time, attack your Queen. You will lose valuable development opportunities because you will have to move your Queen over and over again while your opponent will be properly developing many pieces.

In this position, black has developed the Queen before bringing out any of the black Knights, Bishops, or Rooks. As a result, white has a very strong move, developing the Knight on b1 to c3 (Nb1-c3). The Knight develops to a strong natural square and, at the same time, attacks the Queen. The Queen, a much more valuable piece than the white Knight, will have to move again.

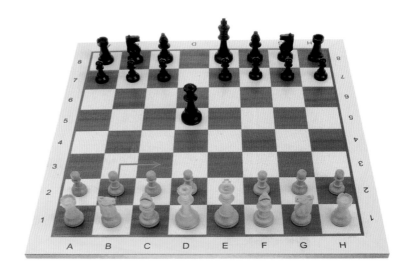

Some players might simply retreat the black Queen to its starting square. Imagine, however, that black decides to move the Queen to e5 giving check (Qd5-e5+). Here, white has responded to the check from the Queen by developing the light-squared Bishop to e2 (Bf1-e2). Then, with white to move, white can bring out another piece, in this case the Knight on g1 to f3 yet again attacking the black Queen. As you can see, white is busy developing pieces actively while black is forced to make moves again and again with the Queen.

Many beginning players have never been told, or simply don't believe, that you shouldn't bring the Queen out early. But, please heed my warning and fight the urge to make an early Queen move.

In this position, white has broken the rule and posted the white Queen very aggressively on just the second move of the game. At first glance, you might wonder why the move is so bad. After all, the Queen attacks the undefended black pawn on e5. The Queen's move, however, offers black a simple way to develop effectively. First, black can defend the e5-pawn by developing the Knight on b8 to c6 (Nb8-c6). On the next move, black can simply advance the g-pawn to g6, gaining time by attacking the Queen and getting ready to develop the Knight from g8 to f6 and the Bishop from f8 to g7.

Safeguard Your Queen

Rather than develop the Queen too early, where it might be a target and assist your opponent's development, try developing all of your other pieces first. That way, your opponent may not be able to figure out what you intend to do with your Queen. Remaining flexible is often a good idea in chess, especially when it comes to developing your Queen.

In this position from a game between two masters, both players have placed their Queens far from the center. Neither Queen can be easily attacked, yet both are likely to aid in the later action.

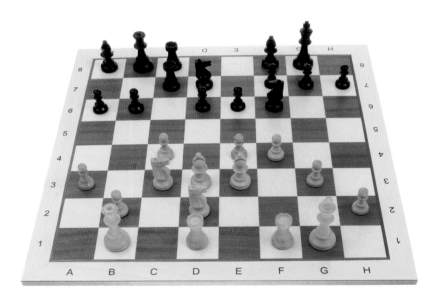

The goal in chess, of course, is checkmate, an attack on the King from which there is no escape. The most important advice, therefore, is to secure your King before you launch your attacks. Masters often spend an extra move or two to make sure that their Kings are safely removed from open files and diagonals before they begin their attacks. They know from experience that complicated maneuvers will often fail because, at the end of a complicated set of moves, an exposed King will be attacked, pinned, or skewered.

In this position, white has dominated the center quickly with pawns on d4 and e4 and developed a Bishop, while black has preferred to fianchetto the Queen's Bishop (see Chapter 5 for more on fianchettos). Seeing an opportunity for a quick attack, black advances the f-pawn to f5 (f7-f5).

White takes advantage of black's poor development by capturing the pawn on f5 (e4xf5). At first glance, it would appear that white has made a terrible mistake. After all, black can now capture the white pawn on g2 with the light-squared Bishop (Bb7xg2). That move certainly looks like it will win the white Rook on h1.

However, white has a very powerful response that takes advantage of the undeveloped black King. White plays the Queen to h5, giving check (Qd1-h5+). As you can see, the King cannot move. Black has no choice but to block the check by advancing the g-pawn (g7-g6).

CONTINUED ON NEXT PAGE

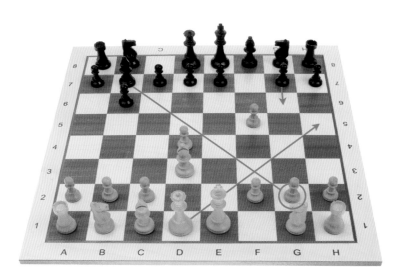

As this next position shows, white has continued the attack by capturing the black g6-pawn with the white pawn on f5 (f5xg6). Black simply does not have time to capture the white Rook on h1 because any move by the white pawn on g6 will be checkmate!

Black therefore decides to develop the Knight on g8 to f6 (Ng8-f6), attacking the white Queen. White now has a fabulous checkmate in two more moves. White continues with pawn take pawn (g6xh7), sacrificing the Queen to the f6 Knight!

Here is the position after black responds with the only possible move, Knight captures Queen (Nf6xh5). White ends the game with the amazing Bishop to g6 checkmate (Bd3-g6#)! This wonderful game emphasizes the need for more rapid development and making sure that your King is safe before your lash out with an attack.

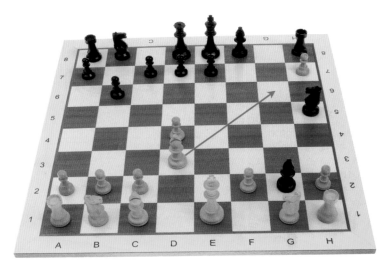

Generally speaking, it is safer to castle on the Kingside (short). Simply put, there is less space to defend. On the Queenside (long), you often have to spend time moving your King at least once more toward the corner. Of course, there are exceptions. If your opponent has castled Kingside, consider castling Queenside in order to launch an attack that includes the advance of the Kingside pawns.

Here, white has castled on the Queenside, while black has castled on the Kingside. White gains an advantage because the white Rook lands on an open file. But the white King has a bit more space to defend. An attack by black on the white a-pawn might require white to move the King again or to advance the a-pawn. And, of course, after castling on the Queenside, the white King is exposed on the c1-h6 diagonal

By contrast, black's King is slightly safer. The King is not exposed to any checks, and all of black's Kingside pawns are defended. However, unlike the white Rook, the black Rook is usually not on an open file after castling on the Kingside.

In this example, white has castled Queenside and taken the added precaution of moving the King further to b1. On c1, the King would rest on a file that black is likely to use to double the black Rooks. By castling on the Queenside, white is able to advance the Kingside pawns forward in a menacing way. White might continue, for example, by advancing the g- or h-pawn again.

Black has castled Kingside here, and is not without possibilities. With black to move, black would likely advance the b-pawn to attack the white Knight (b5-b4). There are good attacking chances for both sides in this position. White will be attempting to coordinate an attack on black's Kingside with moves like g5-g6 and Qd2-h2. Black must not wait for the attack, but rather move aggressively against the white King with moves such as b5-b4, Rf8-c8, and perhaps Nc6-e5-c4.

Don't Push Your Pawns in Front of a Castled King

In Chapter 6, "Pawn Strategy," you learned that every pawn move creates a weakness. This section presents three additional examples that demonstrate the consequence of advancing pawns in front of a castled King.

In this first example, black has advanced the g-pawn (g7-g6). As a result, two squares have become weak: f6 and h6. Both of these are squares that the pawn controlled before moving forward.

White has many different moves that might take advantage of these weaknesses. For example, white might move the Queen to c3 or to h6, threatening to deliver checkmate with the Queen on the g7 square. Or white might simply advance the h-pawn to h5 in an effort to open the h-file and to blow apart the black Kingside. Generally speaking, the more moves made in front of a castled King, the more vulnerable the King will be.

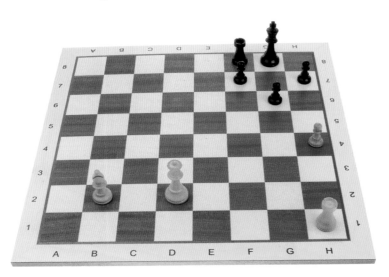

In this second example, black has weakened the Kingside by advancing the h-pawn to h6. As a result, white has at least two plans for breaking through. First, white could simply challenge the black h6-pawn by playing g4 to g5. Note that the white h-pawn, the Rook, and the Queen all support the g4 to g5 advance. But let's consider an interesting alternative. The advance of the black h-pawn has created a short pawn chain. The black h6-pawn is the strong pawn in the chain. By contrast, the black pawn on g7 is the weak pawn in the chain. White might therefore consider the pawn move f5 to f6.

Black's movement of the black g7-pawn to g6 or f6 would permit white to capture the h6-pawn with the Queen. If, instead, black advanced the g-pawn to g5, white could pry apart the Kingside with the h4 to g5 pawn capture (h4xg5). And black's third option of leaving the pawn on g7 would, of course, permit the f6 to g7 pawn capture, (f6xg7). Things don't look good for black.

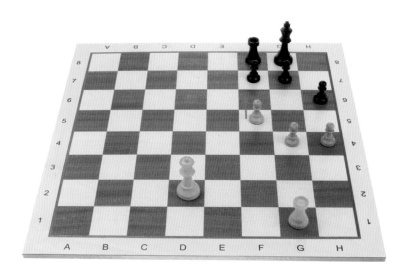

In this last example, black has advanced two pawns in front of the King. Again, the weakness of black's Kingside creates many good options for white. For example, the white Queen might move to d3 or e4 in order to threaten Queen to h7 checkmate. Or the white Queen might move to h5 in order to attack the backward black h-pawn. Or white could simply advance the h-pawn to h4 in an effort to break apart black's pawn structure.

You don't need to remember all of the details. However, you should remember that moving the pawns in front of a castled King exposes the King to many dangers. Advance those pawns at your own peril.

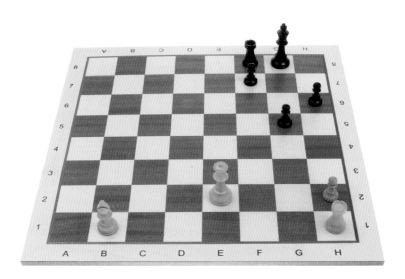

Opening Strategy

Now that you know how to set up the board and how to move and activate the pieces and pawns, it's time to start putting it all together. Playing chess is very much like being a commander in a war. You are in control of all your pieces. Some beginners make the mistake of bringing out only one or two pieces, while leaving the rest of their army on their original squares. To play a good game, it's important to try to coordinate all of the pieces in your army.

In this chapter, you will learn about using all of your pieces to fight for the center the board. You will see why it's important to develop your Knights before your Bishops and why you should limit the number of early pawn moves. If you place your pieces on active squares, you will find that your attacks succeed more often.

Fight for the Center of the Board

The center of the chessboard forms the high ground in a chess battle. If you dominate the center of the board, your attacks are very likely to succeed.

Two Common Opening Moves for White

The absolute center consists of the four squares highlighted here (d4, d5, e4, and e5). From the very beginning of the game, you want to fight for control over these squares.

The two most common first moves for white are pawn e2 to e4 (1.e2-e4) and pawn d2 to d4 (1.d2-d4). These moves have merit. If you open the game with e2 to e4, as in this example, you can see that the pawn already occupies one of the key center squares and exercises control over another central square, d5.

Note: *Remember that a numeral followed by a period in chess notation indicates the move number. For a refresher, see "Chess Notation" in Chapter 1.*

Notice also that the white Bishop on f1 and the white Queen on d1 gain the ability to move out. Although you have already learned not to develop your Queen too early, having these early mobility options often proves useful. For example, black should not reply with the move b7 to b5 (1.b7-b5) because white's Bishop on f1 would be able to capture it.

In addition to staking a claim in the center, white's e2-e4 opening move has an important threat. Here, the threat is simply the move that white would make if white could move again—d2 to d4 (2.d2-d4)—taking full command over the center of the board. The two pawns together, if unopposed, occupy two of the squares in the center and exercise control over the other two center squares.

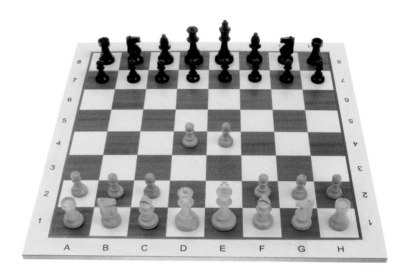

White's other main possibility at the beginning of the game is d2 to d4 (1.d2-d4). Here, too, the pawn occupies one of the central squares and helps control another key square, e5. In this case, the move provides additional mobility for the white Bishop on c1 and carries the obvious second move threat of e2 to e4 (2.e2-e4).

These first moves are bit like a religion: Some players believe firmly in one or the other. Players who prefer e2 to e4 (1.e2-e4) tend to be highly tactical players—players who prefer highly complicated contests that require careful calculation. By contrast, players who open the game with d2 to d4 (1.d2-d4) tend to be more positional players, who prefer a calmer, more strategic approach to chess. In my experience, younger players tend to prefer opening games with 1.e2-e4, and more seasoned players often prefer 1.d2-d4.

An Ideal Setup

You won't always be able to obtain this ideal setup (described in detail below) for your pieces; in fact, the moves that you make will depend on what your opponent does. But the following position represents a goal, an ideal position that you might want to obtain if your opponent puts up very little resistance.

Your Goal

In this position, white has complete command over the center of the board. The two pawns on d4 and e4 occupy two of the squares in the center. White is exercising very strong control over the d5-square. As you can see, the Knight on c3 (Nc3), the Bishop on c4 (Bc4), and the pawn on e4 all help control the key d5-square. White also has excellent control over the key e5-square. The pawn on d4 and the Knight on f3 (Nf3) are both attacking e5.

Place Your Pieces on Their Best Squares

In this ideal setup, white has succeeded in developing every piece. The Rooks occupy the central files and exert influence over the center. Having castled on the Kingside, the white King is safe. Both Bishops have been developed, and the white Queen, while developed, is posted where it will not be easily subject to attack.

Note that white is now fully prepared for the next step—an attack on the black King. For example, the white Bishop on c4 (Bc4) is attacking black's f7-pawn, the weakest spot in black's beginning setup. The f7 pawn is weak because only the black King defends it.

Keep in mind that every move in chess is important. Beginners often make the mistake of moving the same piece or a small number of pieces over and over again. In the early part of the game, try to place your pieces on strong natural squares, squares that will help to control the center or, like the Bc4, control key diagonals. Try not to move a piece more than once or at most twice in the first ten moves of the game . . . unless by doing so you can capture (or recapture) a piece or force your opponent to retreat. In other words, don't start attacking until all or at least most of your pieces are developed.

TIP

Get Online

The Internet offers a full range of chess activities and never-ending opportunities to play. Many websites even provide free instruction. Not surprisingly, my top recommendation is www.queen sac.com, a site that I began nearly 20 years ago. In addition to free instruction, there are thousands of free games to play through.

Another Web gathering place for chess enthusiasts is www.chesscafe.com. Here you'll find instructional articles for beginners, several book reviews, and some fascinating archives for those who enjoy the history of the game.

To improve your tactics and your endgame, visit http://chess.about.com/od/improveyourgame; this site contains numerous exercises.

Knights Before Bishops

As my Uncle Joe used to say, "Knights before Bishops, Knights before Bishops, Knights before Bishops." I think that he said it three times because he really meant it. There are exceptions, but moving Bishops first can cost time later because the Bishop may be posted on a square that in a few moves, if not immediately, could be attacked. So make my uncle happy and move your Knights before you move your Bishops!

Advantages to Developing Knights First

Most of the time, it is fairly clear where the Knights should be developed. The best squares for the Bishops become apparent a bit later. In this position, white has opened the game with e2 to e4 (1.e2-e4). Black, in an effort to prevent white from carrying out the threat of d2 to d4 for it's second move (2.d2-d4), has responded with an opening move of e7 to e5 (1.e7-e5). This popular response is a favorite at chess tournaments.

For its second move, white has several options. Both Knights can develop to their natural squares on c3 and f3. Knight to f3 (2.Ng1-f3) is the preferred response for several reasons. This Knight move attacks the black pawn on e5, and it helps prepare for castling by clearing a square between the King and the h1-Rook. The Knight on f3 also supports the later move d2-d4, an important part of the effort to control the center of the board.

Disadvantages to Developing Bishops First

All of the possible moves by white's light-squared Bishops are considered not as good. Playing Bishop f1 to a6 (2.Bf1-a6) is the worst Bishop move, not because the move does not help white control the center, but because the black pawn on b7 and the black Knight on b8 both control the a6 square. A second move of Bishop f1 to a6 would lose the Bishop!

Note: *You may come across "?" or "??" in chess notation. The "?" indicates a bad move, and "??" a very bad move. Therefore, the Bishop f1 to a6 move detailed above can also be notated as 2.Bf1-a6??.*

A second move of Bishop f1 to d3 (2.Bf1-d3) is also considered very weak. On d3, the Bishop would defend the white e4-pawn, but it also blocks the advance of the important white d-pawn. If the d-pawn can't move, white's dark-squared Bishop on c1 might also have a difficult time entering the game.

Even Bishop f1 to b5 (2.Bf1-b5) is considered a poor second move because black will be able to play either pawn a7 to a6 (2.a7-a6) or even pawn c7 to c6 (2.c7-c6), attacking the Bishop and forcing it to move again. Your goal with the Bishops is to place them on strong natural squares. If it isn't clear which Bishop move is best, you will want to wait until you have a clear reason why one move might be better than the others.

Here, white has played Knight g1 to f3 (2.Ng1-f3), attacking black's e5-pawn. Black has responded to the threat by playing Knight b8 to c6 (2.Nb8-c6). As you can see, the black Knight on c6 defends the black e5-pawn. In this position, white is finally ready to consider moving the Bishop on f1 (Bf1). Many players try Bishop f1 to c4 (3.Bf1-c4), preparing to castle by clearing the squares between the King and h1-Rook and beginning to place pressure on the weak f7-square. (Remember, the f7-pawn is weak because only the King is defending it.) The best third move for white, however, is probably Bishop f1 to b5 (3.Bf1-b5). It is a move that was bad just a move ago. But now, the Bishop arrives on b5 with an attack on the black Knight on c6 (Nc6), all with the idea of putting more pressure on the black e5-pawn. White's idea is simple enough. Perhaps, by capturing the black c6-Knight (Bb5xc6), white will be able to win the black pawn on e5 in its fourth move. Black will be busy responding with a Bishop recapture (b7xc6 or d7xc6) for its third move.

Quick development is one of the main keys to success in chess. The winner of the game is often the player who, after just ten moves, has the most pieces bearing down on the center. With that in mind, early pawn moves that do not have a bearing on the center could be a waste of time.

Avoid Early Maneuvers on the Flank

Certainly, early in the game, try to limit the number of moves made by pawns on the a-, b-, g-, and h-files (these files are called *flanks* because they're on the outside edges of the board). The following example is a bit extreme. White began by playing g2 to g4 (1.g2-g4) and has continued by advancing the f-pawn (2.f2-f3). Black can punish such play very quickly, in this case with a Queen to h4 checkmate (2.Qd8-h4#)—the fastest possible mate.

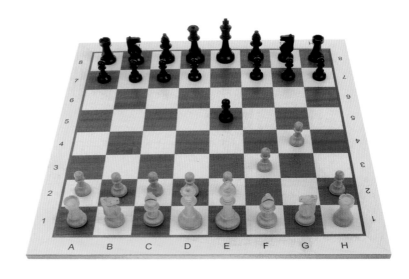

Very few players will fall into that quick check-mate. Here is a more practical example. Black, a beginner, has developed only on the flanks. White, a more experienced player, has taken quick control over the center, castled, and even developed a Rook to the e-file. By contrast, black has no control over the center other than two attacks from the Bishops. Black would also like to castle on the Kingside in order to safeguard the King, but to do so, the black Knight on g8 (Ng8) would have to move first. The natural move, of course, is Knight on g8 to f6 (Ng8-f6). However, the strong white pawn center makes that move very hard to play, as explained on the next page.

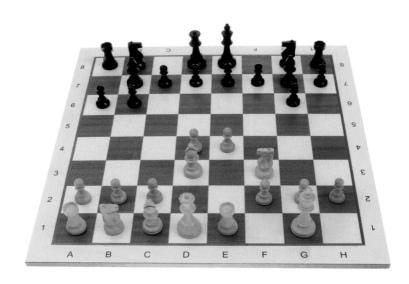

Here is the position after Knight g8 to f6 (Ng8-f6). White can respond powerfully with pawn e4 to e5 (e4-e5), taking further command over the center and forcing the poor f6-Knight (Nf6) to move again. Notice that if the Knight moves again to d5, g4, or h5, it will be subject to another attack from a white pawn.

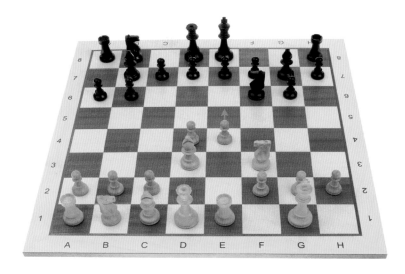

The worst of these choices is perhaps Knight to h5 (Nf6-h5). By moving to h5, the Knight has moved to the rim and no longer has any safe moves. White might be reluctant to weaken the position in front of the King, but the attacking move pawn g2-g4 (g2-g4) will win the Knight. Like many games, chess has its tradeoffs. In this instance, the capture of the black Knight should compensate white for the weakening of the Kingside.

The real point, of course, is to fight for the center and to avoid early maneuvers on the flank that cede the center to your opponent.

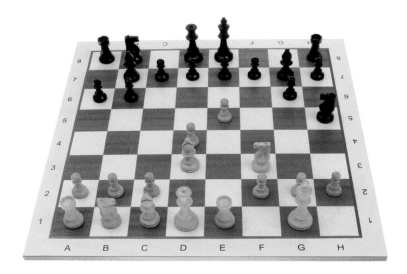

Complete Your Development Before You Attack

All too often, beginners tend to begin their attacks before they have completed developing their pieces. Be sure to develop first, then attack.

Develop First

Here is a typical example of such a mistake. In this position, white probably should develop the Knight from b1 to c3 (Nb1-c3), or simply castle. Instead, white launches an aggressive attack on the black Kingside with Knight from f3 to g5 (Nf3-g5). White sees that having the Knight on g5 (Ng5), and the white Bishop on c4 (Bc4) will combine to attack the black f7-pawn twice. For the moment, at least, black has only a single defender of f7, the black King.

Here is the position after black's response, castling Kingside. As you can see, by castling, black now defends the key f7-pawn twice, with the Rook on f8 (Rf8) as well as the King. Intent on the attack, white mistakenly lashes forward, moving the Knight yet again to capture on f7 (Nf3xf7). Black will respond, capturing the white Knight with its Rook (Rf8xf7), and then white answers by capturing the black Rook with its c4-Bishop, putting the King in check (Bc4xf7+). The black King then captures the white Bishop (Kg8xf7). The trade of two minor pieces, in this case a Knight and a Bishop, for a Rook and pawn is rarely a good idea so early in the game. See the next position below for how this plays out.

After the captures have cleared on f7, black's position is well developed. The two Knights are on natural squares, c6 and f6, helping to control the center. The Bishop on c5 (Bc5) is also well placed. Black is likely to continue development with pawn d7 to d6 (d7-d6), bringing the Bishop from c8 to e6 (Bc8-e6), retreating the King back to g8 for safety (Kf7-g8), and then finding files for the Queen and the remaining Rook, probably on the f-file.

By clear contrast, white's development has suffered. Both Rooks, the Knight, the Bishop, and the Queen are—as masters like to say— still "in the box;" they haven't moved from their starting positions. White has made very little progress, while black has an excellent plan to activate every piece.

The cause of this catastrophe for white was the premature attack on f7. Rather than lash out by moving the same piece three times in the opening, white should simply have tried to develop slowly, bringing out all or most of the pieces before commencing the attack.

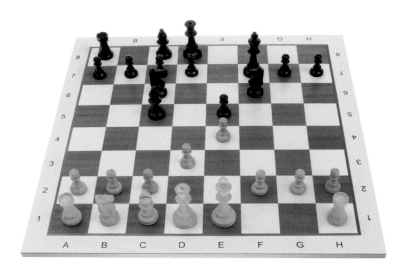

Gain Time

As you are developing, pay attention to your opponent's moves. Is your opponent threatening to capture one of your pieces? Did your opponent leave a piece undefended where it can be successfully captured at little or no cost to you? Almost as important, can you gain time by forcing your opponent to retreat?

Alekhine's Defense

In this position, black has responded to white's opening move of pawn e2 to e4 (1.e2-e4) with the very sharp Knight g8 to f6 (1.Ng8-f6). This opening—known as *Alekhine's Defense,* after former world champion Alexander Alekhine—prevents white from playing a second move of pawn d2 to d4 (2.d2-d4) because black's first move threatens to capture the white pawn on e4.

White could decide to defend the e4-pawn with pawn d2 to d3 (2.d2-d3), but the white d-pawn really would like to develop directly to d4. White therefore decides to gain time by advancing the e-pawn for a second time to e5 (e4-e5). The second advance of the white e-pawn might appear to break the rule of developing a piece only once, but the advance does present the black Knight with a problem.

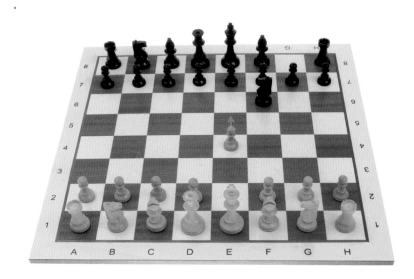

Black mistakenly advances the attacked Knight to e4 (Nf6-e4). Knight f6 to d5 (Nf6-d5) is the main line, although the Knight can also be attacked there by the white pawns. In this position, white can continue to attack the black Knight with its d2-pawn (3.d2-d3), gaining time for rapid development. Here is the position after the third moves by white (d2-d3) and black (Ne4-c5). (These moves can be notated together as 3.d2-d3 Ne4-c5).

Note: *When both white's move and black's move are notated together, they are preceded by the move number, with white's move always being listed first, as above.*

The poor black Knight is being forced to move again and again, while white is successfully establishing a strong pawn center. White's next move is likely to be d3 to d4 (4.d3-d4), followed by the rapid deployment of the white Knights to f3 and c3.

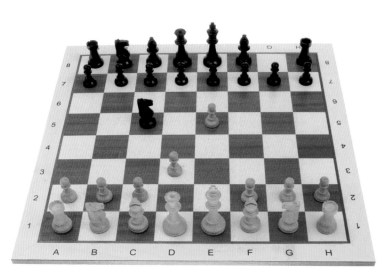

Many beginners feel that they ought to exchange pieces—Knights for Knights, Bishops for Bishops, Rooks for Rooks—whenever they have the opportunity. As a general rule, exchanges are not often advantageous because they only help an opponent gain time for development.

Avoid Early Exchanges

In this position, both sides have been developing normally, bringing out their Knights first. With white to move, white has an opportunity to exchange Knights on c6 or to develop a Bishop. The best move is probably to develop the Bishop on f1 to c4 (Bf1-c4). If, instead, white decides to capture the black Knight on c6 (Nd4xc6), black will simply recapture with the b7-pawn (b7xc6) and gain time for development. The pawn on c6 would be useful in supporting the later advance of the black d-pawn.

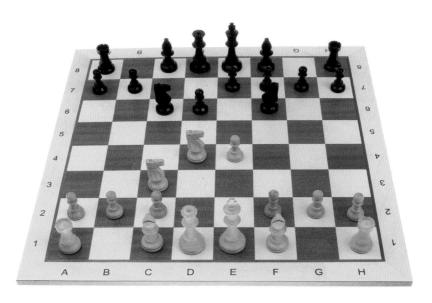

CONTINUED ON NEXT PAGE

It is possible that white feared that black would exchange Knights on d4. Here is the position after the white Bishop moves from f1 to c4 (6.Bf1-c4) and the exchange of Knights on d4. It is true that white, in recapturing on d4, had to develop the Queen aggressively and early (Qd1xNd4). Notice, however, that black does not have a useful, immediate way to attack the white Queen. The black pawn move of e7 to e5 (7.e7-e5) permanently weakens the d6-pawn and creates a hole at d5. If black instead moves the Queen from d8 to b6 (7.Qd8-b6) white can exchange Queens, which will in turn result in doubled black pawns on the b-file.

In Many Openings, One Exchange Is Useful

Waiting for your opponent to do the exchanging is usually good because most recapturing often improves your position. In many openings, however, one exchange is advantageous. In this position, white opened with e2 to e4 (1.e2-e4), and black responded with e7 to e6 (1.e7-e6), the *French Defense*. The idea behind the French Defense is to delay the fight for the center by one move.

Note: *In the early 1800s, a Paris team used this opening move to defeat a London team in a correspondence match, thus the name French Defense. For more on correspondence chess, see page 134 in Chapter 10.*

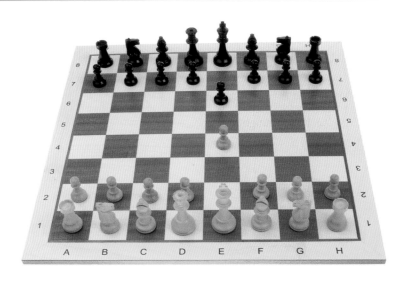

As you can see, black made no effort to prevent white from taking full command over the center. So white proceeds with the usual strategy, playing pawn d2 to d4 (2.d2-d4). Black responds immediately with d7 to d5 (2.d7-d5), a move that instantly places pressure on the white e4-pawn.

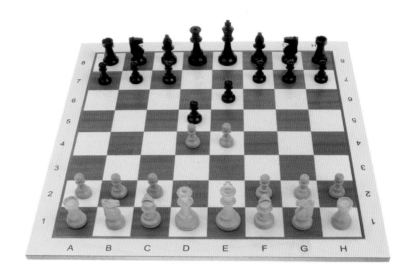

Following the idea of limiting exchanges, white declines to capture the pawn on d5 (3.e4xd5). Rather, white pursues straightforward development with the b1-Knight to c3 (3.Nb1-c3), defending the e4-pawn and placing additional pressure on black's d5-pawn. Black responds with the *Classical Variation of the French Defense,* developing it's g8-Knight to f6 (3.Ng8-f6). With a Knight on f6, black places more pressure on the white e4-pawn.

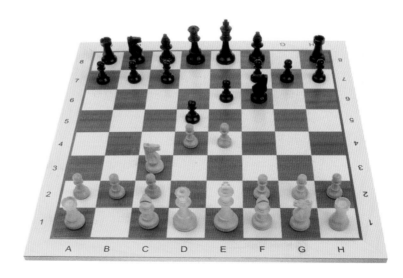

CONTINUED ON NEXT PAGE

In this position, white has an important choice. White could push the e-pawn from e4 to e5 (e4-e5), establishing a small pawn chain on d4 and e5. If white were to do that, its light-squared Bishop would become good. White's dark-squared Bishop, however, would become bad (trapped by the fixed pawns on the d4 and e5 dark squares). At the same time, black's light-squared Bishop on c8 would become bad, trapped by its own pawns, while black's dark-squared Bishop would become good.

Note: For a refresher on good and bad Bishops, see Chapter 5, "Bishop Strategy."

White's interest is in trying to exchange the bad Bishop on g5 (Bg5) for black's good dark-squared Bishop. To prevent the loss of the Knight, black "unpins" with its Bishop, moving it from f8 to e7 (Bf8-e7). On g5, the white Bishop is pinning the black Knight on f6 and threatening to play e4-e5, attacking and perhaps winning the pinned Knight.

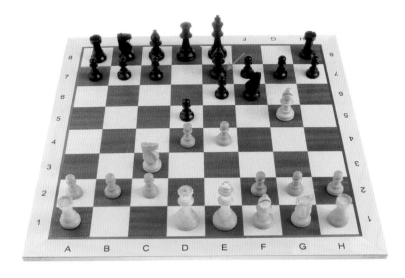

Now, of course, after white advances its e4 pawn to e5 (5.e4-e5) and the black Knight retreats from f6 to d7 (5.Nf6-d7), white will succeed in exchanging the bad dark-squared Bishop for black's good Bishop.

As you have seen, Bishops can dominate Knights, and Bishops tend to be more useful than Knights so long as the board is not sealed shut by long-fixed pawn structures. Exchanging a Bishop for a Knight too early in the game is a very risky strategy, even if the exchange brings about doubled pawns. The reason is that, early in the game, the pawn structure is not yet set. The person with the extra Bishop can aim to keep the board open so their extra Bishop will be able to work well.

Here is a position early in a game after white opens d2 to d4, black opens Knight g8 to f6, and white responds Bishop c1 to g5 (1.d2-d4 Ng8-f6 2.Bc1-g5). This opening, called *the Trompowski*, breaks the important rule of developing a Bishop before the Knights. White's strategy, perhaps flawed, is to weaken the black pawn structure by capturing the black Knight on f6.

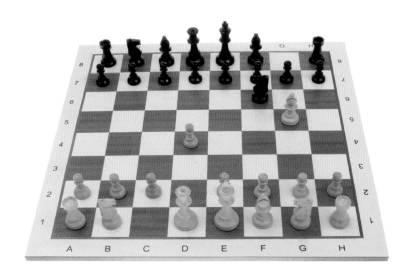

Here is the same game a few moves later. Note that the black f-pawns are indeed doubled. In compensation, black has aggressively posted the dark-squared Bishop on g7. This Bishop is quite strong because it is well posted on the long diagonal and because white no longer has a dark-squared Bishop to challenge it. Black may not be able to castle safely on the Kingside, but black could later in the game be able to post a Rook or even double Rooks on the open g-file. Note also that black's f5-pawn is preventing white from developing normally with e3-e4.

The point, of course, is that such early exchanges of Bishops for Knights are very committal and might determine who will have winning chances. It's best to avoid such exchanges if you have the Bishop and, of course, to seek such exchanges if you have the Knight.

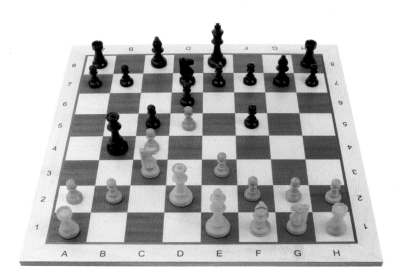

Opening Variations

The beginning moves of a chess game, the first phase of the game, are called the opening. Some players spend years memorizing long opening variations, but you can get far in chess with a firm understanding of just a few key principles. Make sure that you fight for control of the center of the board. In your fight for the center, try to limit the number of your pawn moves. Before you attack, try to develop most of your pieces on squares that help control the center and from which they can't easily be attacked. In other words, pick safe, good squares for your pieces, and don't keep moving one piece if you have many other pieces that have not been moved.

Of course, don't play like a robot. You can have a good plan or idea for where all your pieces may go, but carefully watch the moves that your opponent makes. If your opponent makes a move that threatens something, it's often best to eliminate that threat before you continue with your development. Most of the openings in this section conform to these principles. I have also included a set of bad openings that break these rules. As you will see, there are good reasons to avoid such moves.

One more thing: In previous chapters, I described moves with both text (move the Knight on b4 to c2) and with chess notation (Nb4-c2). In this chapter through the end of the book, you'll see that I mainly use chess notation to identify pieces and to describe moves. Review the "Chess Notation" section in Chapter 1 for a refresher on this notation.

A number of interesting openings begin with the moves 1.e2-e4 e7-e5. This is called a *double King pawn opening* because King's pawns (the pawn directly in front of each King) advance two squares. Black's first move prevents white from establishing a broad pawn center with pawns on e4 and d4. Like white's first move, 1.e7-e5 provides the black Bishop on f8 (Bf8) and the black Queen with some mobility.

Alternatives to 2.Ng1-f3

In this common opening position, white has several logical ideas for its second move. I examine the most common choice, 2.Ng1-f3, just below. In this section, I introduce several interesting alternatives for white. The King's Gambit offers a pawn in exchange for quick development. The Vienna Game offers a tamer alternative that will permit you to develop quickly. The Center Game is a less favored choice because white's Queen enters the game too early.

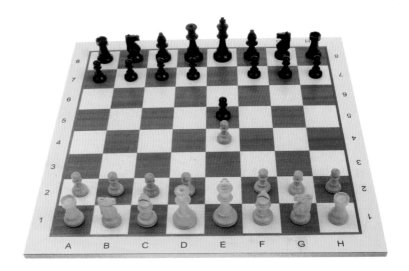

KING'S GAMBIT (1.E2-E4 E7-E5 2.F2-F4

The famous *King's Gambit* continues with 2.f2-f4. Black, of course, will often simply capture the pawn on f4 with e5xf4. Gambits are openings that offer material, here the white pawn on f4, in exchange for space or rapid development. As a result of the capture on f4, black takes a material advantage, the extra pawn on f4. White offers the f-pawn in the King's Gambit in an effort to obtain immediate control over the center with 3.Ng1-f3 and 4.d2-d4. Black has interesting ideas here as well. If white does not play 3.Ng1-f3, black could try the very aggressive 3.Qd8-h4+. If white does play 3.Ng1-f3, black can play 3.g7-g5, a move that breaks the rule about fighting for the center but the move does hold on to the extra pawn and it threatens 4.g5-g4.

Note: *The King's Gambit, defined by the moves 1.e2-e4 e7-e5 2. f2-f4 was a favorite opening choice during the 19th century. It remains appealing because, at the cost of only a pawn, white gains full control over the center with d2-d4 as well as an open f-file.*

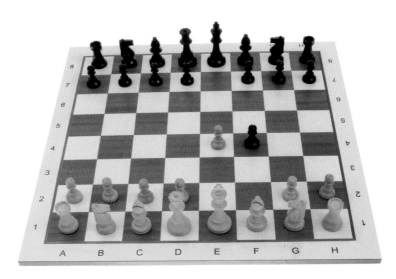

THE VIENNA GAME (1.E2-E4 E7-E5 2.NB1-C3)

The *Vienna Game*, 2.Nb1-c3, is another option. Rather than offer the f-pawn with 2.f2-f4, white prepares the advance of the f-pawn with moves such as 3.Bf1-c4, 4.d2-d3, and *then* 5.f2-f4, when white's Bishop (Bc1) would be able to recapture on f4.

Note: *The Vienna Game, defined by the moves 1.e2-e4 e7-e5 2.Nb1-c3 is a cousin of the King's Gambit. Rather than play 2.f2-f4 immediately, white postpones the move in the hope of getting more pieces developed before the attack starts.*

The disadvantage of the Vienna Game is that white's second move does not contain an immediate threat. Black can therefore respond aggressively with 2.Ng8-f6. If white continues with the plan of 3.Bf1-c4, black has an interesting tactical shot.

CONTINUED ON NEXT PAGE

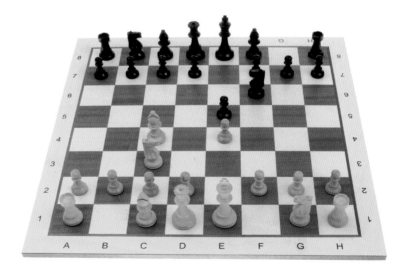

Black can play 3.Nf6xe4 because, if white recaptures on e4 with 4.Nc3xe4, black can recover a piece with an amazing pawn fork. As you can see in this diagram, the pawn move 4.d7-d5 is attacking both the Bishop (Bc4) and the Knight (Ne4).

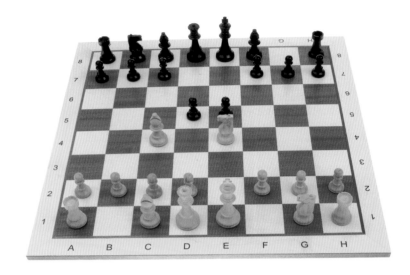

Of course, white wasn't required to recapture on e4. Instead, the most interesting move for white is the very aggressive 4.Qd1-h5. In this position, white is already threatening checkmate on f7, as well as to recapture the white Knight on e4. Black would need to retreat Ne4-d6 to stop both threats with an interesting and complex game ahead.

THE CENTER GAME (1.E2-E4 E7-E5 2.D2-D4)

The *Center Game* is a relatively poor opening choice for white. Although white's second move does place pressure on the center, white will find that, after black counters with 2.e5xd4, there is simply no good way to recapture. Recapturing the d4-pawn with 3.Qd1xd4 places the white Queen prematurely in the center where it will be easy for black to attack with Nb8-c6. As you might imagine, an early Ng1-f3 would have improved white's plan, because the Knight on f3 rather than the Queen would then be able to recapture on d4.

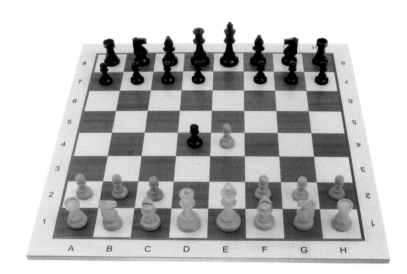

Continuing with 2.Ng1-f3

The most common second move for white after 1.e2-e4 e7-e5 is simply to develop the Knight on g1 to f3 (Ng1-f3). The Knight move threatens to capture the black pawn on e5, develops the Knight to a logical square that exerts influence over two central squares (d4 and e5), helps to prepare the advance of the white d-pawn to d4, and the move brings white a little closer to castling. The openings in this section all begin with 2.Ng1-f3.

THE RUY LOPEZ (1.E2-E4 E7-E5 2.NG1-F3 NB8-C6 3.BF1-B5)

For the reasons stated just above, most players find that 2.Ng1-f3 is the most logical second move for white. Black's most common response is to defend the black e5-pawn by playing Nb8-c6.

CONTINUED ON NEXT PAGE

White's third move, 3.Bf1-b5, defines the opening as the *Ruy Lopez,* or the Spanish game. The Bishop on b5 threatens to capture the black Knight that is defending the black e-pawn. Just as important, the Bishop move prepares white to castle on the Kingside and then to bring the King's Rook to e1, where it will exert significant support for the center.

Note: *A Spanish priest named Ruy Lopez wrote at length about this opening in 1561. The opening remains popular today and is regularly revitalized by the strongest players with fresh analysis. The opening maintains the pressure on the black center and often leads to a complex struggle for control over the center of the board.*

In the Ruy Lopez, white will often proceed very slowly, preparing the move d2-d4. Here is an ideal setup for white in the Ruy Lopez. Note that white has prepared the advance d2-d4 with c2-c3. If black were to capture on d4, white would recapture with the c3-pawn, maintaining a strong pawn center. Note also that white's Queen's Knight has reached the g3-square, where it usefully supports the white pawn on e4 and aims to advance aggressively with Ng3-f5.

To get to the g3 square, the Knight followed the interesting path Nb1-d2-f1-g3, a very common maneuver in the Ruy Lopez. Finally, note that black "kicked" the white Bishop on b5 back to b3 with both a7 to a6 and then with b7 to b5. This Bishop is sometimes called the *Ruy Bishop.* If white succeeds in advancing the center pawns, this Bishop can become a very powerful force in assisting attacks on black's Kingside. If the central pawns become fixed, this "Ruy Bishop" could remain bad.

THE SCOTCH GAME (1.E2-E4 E7-E5 2.NG1-F3 NB8-C6 3.D2-D4)

White does not have to play 3.Bf1-b5. On the third move, white has the choice of entering the *Scotch game* with 3.d2-d4. Unlike the Ruy Lopez, in which white carefully prepares the d2-d4 advance, in the Scotch game, white plays the move straight away. The move often leads to quick exchanges that can limit white's attacking chances, which is the main reason strong chess players prefer the Ruy Lopez to the Scotch game.

Note: *The Scotch game received its name from a correspondence chess game played between Edinburgh and London in 1824. A 19th century favorite of Grandmasters Blackburne and Chigorin, the opening has been played more and more lately by the best players.*

PETROV'S DEFENSE (1.E2-E4 E7-E5 2.NG1-F3 NG8-F6)

Rather than defending the e-pawn on the second move, black has the option of coun- terattacking with *Petrov's Defense*. As you can see, like white, black has also developed the King's Knight, ignoring the attack on the e5- pawn, and instead countering with an attack on the white e4-pawn. At first glance, it would seem that each side now has the opportunity to capture a pawn. White can play 3.Nf3xe5 and black could respond with 3.Nf6xe4.

Note: *Petrov's Defense is named after Alexander Petrov, a 19th-century Russian chess player. An alternative spelling is Petroff's Defense, and in Europe, it's sometimes called the Russian game.*

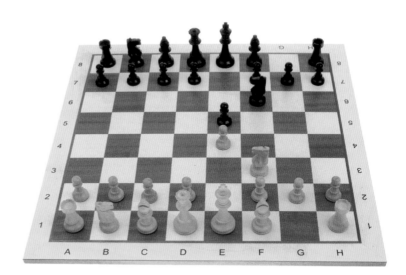

CONTINUED ON NEXT PAGE

In this position, both players have captured a pawn but white also has a very strong response with 4.Qd1-e2. Note that the two Knight captures have completely opened up the e-file. With the move 4.Qd1-e2, white immediately threatens to capture the undefended black Knight on e4.

Black cannot continue to copy white's moves because, after 4.Qd8-e7, the white Queen will successfully capture the black Knight on e4.

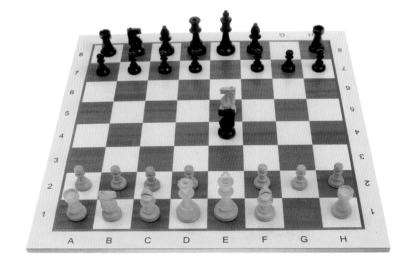

Black has an enormous problem in this position. If black moves the Knight on e4 away, say to f6, white will be able to take full advantage of the open e-file with a powerful discovered check.

The best move for white after black's 4.Ne4-f6 is the amazing 5.Ne5-c6, revealing a check from the Queen. The discovered check will, no matter what black does, result in the loss of the black Queen to the white Knight!

Correct Play in Petrov's Defense

Rather than copy white's capture in the center, black must first attack the advanced white Knight. Here, black has played the essential move, 3.d7-d6, attacking the white Knight on e5 and forcing it to move away. Once the Knight moves off, black will be able to capture successfully on e4 without having to face the devastating discovered check.

After white's 1.e2-e4 opening, black is not obligated to play 1.e7-e5. In fact, many of the alternative replies in this section are among the most popular choices. Black can choose from dynamic openings such as the *Sicilian*, the *French*, the *Caro-Kann*, and *Alekhine's Defense*.

The Sicilian Defense (1.e2-e4 c7-c5)

Black's first move, 1.c7-c5, defines the opening as a *Sicilian.* Black's move is aggressive. It immediately aims to prevent white from taking command over the center with d2-d4. With just one move, black intends to capture white's central pawn when it reaches d4 and, by so doing, open up the c-file for activity with black's Rooks.

Note: *The Sicilian Defense received its name in the 17th century from the Italian master Greco. Today, the Sicilian is a regular guest at every chess tournament and a favorite of Grandmasters like Bobby Fischer and Garry Kasparov.*

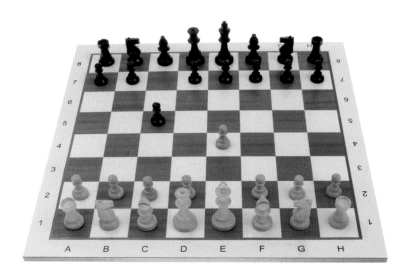

In the Sicilian, white usually develops actively with 2.Ng1-f3 and then 3.d2-d4. When black captures on d4 with the c5-pawn, white intends to recapture with the Knight on f3 rather than the Queen.

Here is a typical Sicilian position after just five moves by each side. White has played d2-d4 and, after a pawn capture, recaptured with a Knight from f3. Both sides have developed their other Knights to posts that help to exert some control over the center. Black has also played the move d7-d6 in an effort to develop the Bishop on c8 and to exert additional control over the e5-square.

Notice that black's c-file is now open. Black's plan might be to develop the Bishop Bf8-e7 (with e7-e6 first or to g7 with g7-g6 first), and then to castle on the Kingside. Within the next dozen moves, or so, black would hope to have doubled Rooks on the c-file.

The French Defense (1.e2-e4 e7-e6)

In the *French Defense,* with 1.e7-e6, black makes no immediate effort to prevent white from playing 2.d2-d4. Here is the basic position in the French Defense after just two moves by each player. As you can see, white has placed both central pawns on their best squares. Black has countered with one pawn in the center, the d5-pawn, supported by the e6-pawn.

Note: *For an explanation of how this defense got it's name, please see "Limit Exchanges" in Chapter 8. Advocates of the French Defense are a loyal bunch, sticking with their approach despite the cramped nature of its positions.*

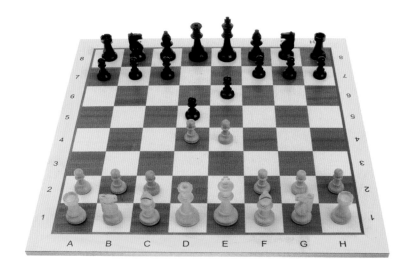

Most positions in the French Defense involve an immediate or slightly delayed e4-e5 pawn push by white. Note that, in this position, the black Bishop on c8 is a bad Bishop because it is already trapped by its own fixed pawns on e6 and d5. Note also that both sides have fixed pawn chains. White would like to proceed aggressively against the black Kingside with moves such as Ng1-f3, Bf1-d3, and perhaps even h2-h4 and Rh1-h3.

Black would likely play against the relative weak d4-pawn and break up white's central pawn chain by playing c7-c5 and then Nb8-c6. Both sides have active and interesting play.

CONTINUED ON NEXT PAGE

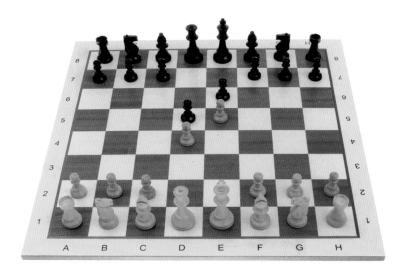

The Caro-Kann Defense (1.e2-e4 c7-c6)

In a strategy very similar to the French Defense, black delays the fight against white's center for one move, but this time beginning with 1.c7-c6, the *Caro-Kann Defense.* As you can see, black has again used a pawn to support the d7-d5 pawn push on black's second move. In one key respect, the Caro-Kann is better than the French Defense because the black pawns do not imprison the black Bishop on c8. Indeed, in this opening, black's light-squared Bishop will be able to play a much more active role than its counterpart in the French Defense.

Note: The Caro-Kann was little understood and barely played until the 1890s when H. Caro of Berlin and M. Kann of Vienna began to play it regularly. World Champion Jose Capablanca used it in a 1922 match. Other World Champions, notably Tigran Petrosian and Anatoly Karpov, have been advocates of the Caro-Kann.

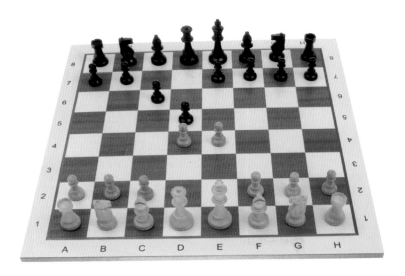

Here is a typical position in the Caro-Kann after just four moves. Black has captured in the center with d5xe4, and the white Knight, which entered the game on c3, has recaptured. Black has taken advantage of the Caro-Kann pawn structure to activate the light-squared Bishop from c8 to f5. As you can see, this Bishop is far more active than the Bishop in the French Defense. In this position, white must either defend or move the currently undefended Knight on e4. The most commonly played move for white here is to retreat the Knight to g3, attacking the black Bishop on f5 and forcing black to retreat it— most commonly to g6.

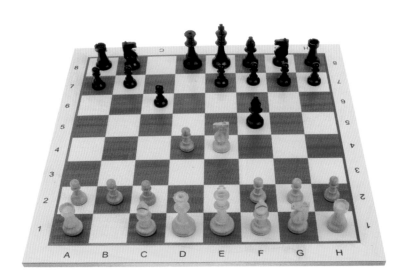

Note that, in this position after the white Knight plays Ne4-g3 and the black Bishop moves Bf5-g6, the black Bishop winds up three squares away from the white Knight. As you saw in Chapter 5, "Bishop Strategy," Bishops can dominate Knights in this manner. A typical white plan from this position involves the idea of a quick flank attack with h2-h4, threatening to trap the Bg6 with h4-h5. Black can respond by making "luft" (the German word for space) for its Bishop with h7-h6.

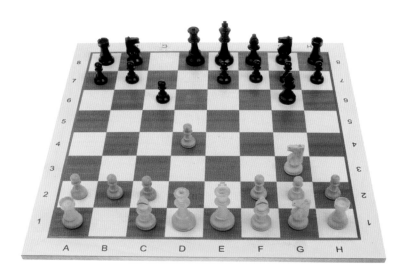

Alekhine's Defense

Alekhine's Defense, named after former world champion Alexander Alekhine, is not for beginners. On the very first move, black prevents white from playing 2.d2-d4 by challenging the white e4-pawn directly. As you saw in Chapter 8, white should proceed in this position by pushing the e-pawn to e5, forcing the Knight to move again. The correct response for black is Nf6-d5.

CONTINUED ON NEXT PAGE

Already on move two, the unusual character of Alekhine's Defense is clear. Black is trying to provoke many pawn moves, while white would like to gain full control over the center and prove that black's strategy of moving the Knight over and over is fatally flawed. In this position after move two, white already has two excellent alternatives: to gain more control over the center with 3.d2-d4 or to challenge black's Knight yet again with 3.c2-c4.

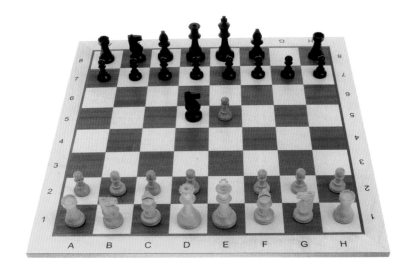

Here is a common position in Alekhine's Defense, an opening variation known as the *Four Pawns Attack*. After white's c2-c4 move, the black Knight retreated once again, this time to b6. White will likely continue with development moves such as Nb1-c3 and Ng1-f3. Few beginners would be happy with the black position, although, in tournament experience, white often finds it difficult to defend all of the forward pawns.

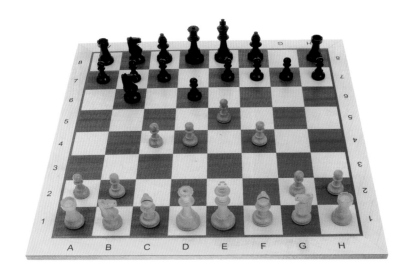

After 1.d2-d4, white is already threatening to take full command over the center with 2.e2-e4. Most of black's replies therefore attempt to prevent white from playing 2.e2-e4. Double Queen pawn openings (moving the pawns located in front the Queens) all involve the black reply 1.d7-d5. White's usual plan in this opening is to prepare e2-e4. Unfortunately, the obvious 2.Nb1-c3 move is not effective because black can defend the e4-square with Ng8-f6.

The Queen's Gambit Accepted

White usually continues with 2.c2-c4, a move that gambits a pawn, though it is rare that black accepts the offer. After 2.c2-c4 d5xc4, white is able to gain undisputed control over the center of the board with 3.Nb1-c3 and 4.e2-e4. Indeed, once white develops normally, it might be able to recapture on c4 with the Bf1. To prevent that, black might have to play moves such as a7-a6 and b7-b5. So many pawn moves on the flank will only encourage white to take full command over the center.

Note: *The Queen's Gambit dates back to 1490, but the opening was considered dull and unambitious. The Queen's gambit began to emerge as a reasonable choice only in 1870s when many players seemed to tire of the already over-analyzed King's Gambit.*

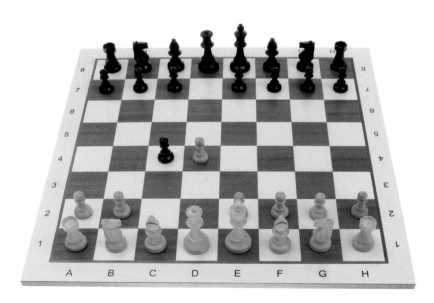

CONTINUED ON NEXT PAGE

Queen's Gambit Declined (1.d2-d4 d7-d5 2.c2-c4 e7-e6 3.Nb1-c3 Ng8-f6)

Most players prefer to decline the gambit and to fight for a share of the center. Here is a typical position in the *Queen's Gambit Declined* after just three moves. White has continued with c2-c4 and then Nb1-c3, which is pressuring the d5-square. Black has responded to this pressure by developing first with e7-e6 and then Ng8-f6.

White would like to play e2-e4, but the black d5-pawn and the black Knight both control the key e4-square. White usually continues with Bc1-g5 in an effort to pin the black Knight and then to play e2-e4. Reacting to the threat, black will usually break the pin with Bf8-e7.

This position has some resemblance to the French Defense in that black's light-squared Bishop is blocked in by the black pawns on e6 and d5. This bad Bishop is one of the main drawbacks for black in the Queen's Gambit Declined.

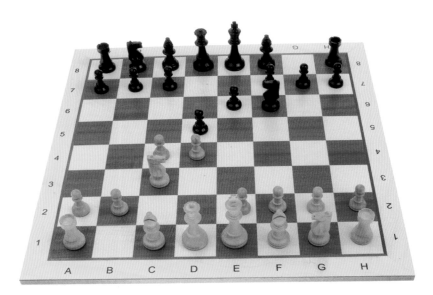

The Slav Defense (1.d2-d4 d7-d5 2.c2-c4 c7-c6)

The *Slav Defense* is very similar to the Queen's Gambit Declined except that black defends the d5-pawn by playing c7-c6 rather than e7-e6. As you can see in this position, black has avoided the problem of sealing in the Bishop on c8. In this respect, the Slav Defense is also similar to the Caro-Kann Defense.

Note: *The Slav gained its name because it was first played by Slavic masters, notably Alapin. Its strength and versatility were unrecognized until grandmaster Euwe adopted it as a regular defense in the 1930s.*

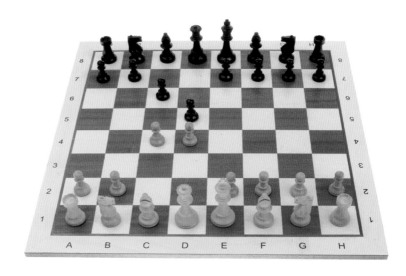

In the Slav, black will usually be able to develop the c8-Bishop aggressively on f5 or g4. In this position, a typical one that might be reached from either the Queen's Gambit, the Queen's Gambit Declined, or the Slav Defense, black has elected instead to fianchetto the Bishop on b7. The black Bishop on b7 is much less active than white's light-squared Bishop on d3. Note that, with the black pawn on c6, the Knight on b8 developed to d7 rather than to c6.

As you can see, black is making it difficult for white to play the attacking move e3-e4. The pawn on d5 and the Knight on f6 stand ready to capture on e4, and black hopes for counter-play with the aggressive move c6-c5, freeing the Bishop on b7.

Indian Defenses

There are other popular ways after white's 1.d2-d4 to prevent white from playing 2.e2-e4. The most common first move today for black against 1.d2-d4 is 1.Ng8-f6. The Knight move by itself prevents 2.e2-e4 and keeps many options alive for black. The popular *King's Indian Defense* involves a Kingside fianchetto by black. The *Queen's Indian Defense* involves a Queenside fianchetto. And the *Nimzo-Indian Defense* is a hard-hitting counter that immediately challenges the white setup.

King's Indian Defense (1.d2-d4 Ng8-f6 2.c2-c4 g7-g6 3.Nb1-c3 Bf8-g7)

In the *King's Indian Defense*, white proceeds with the idea of 2.c2-c4 and 3.Nb1-c3. Black, in turn, pursues a Kingside fianchetto. After just three moves, it has become clear that black's defense does not prevent white from playing 4.e2-e4. White will therefore be able to achieve a broad pawn center.

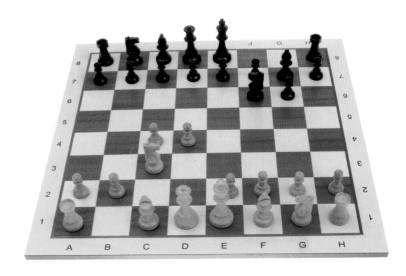

This typical position in the King's Indian pro-vides a sense of the opening's unusual char-acter. Black has challenged white's pawn center by advancing the e-pawn and later the f-pawn. Black is likely to attack on the Kingside in spite of the fact that its King is castled there.

White has achieved much more central space and often attacks on the Queenside with the idea later of c4-c5. The black Knight that opened the game at f6 has moved to the h5 square first to prepare f7-f5 and to make room for the other black Knight, which arrived at f6 from b8 and then d7. See Chapter 10 for a related opening formation—the King's Indian Attack.

Queen's Indian Defense (1.d2-d4 Ng8-f6 2.c2-c4 e7-e6 3.Ng1-f3 b7-b6)

The *Queen's Indian Defense* involves a fianchetto on the Queenside. Here is the position in the Queen's Indian after just three moves. White has again opened with d2-d4 and then c2-c4. Black has countered with 1.Ng8-f6, 2.e7-e6, and then 3.b7-b6. Black intends to play Bc8-b7 where the Bishop, in conjunction with the Knight on f6, tries to prevent white from playing e2-e4.

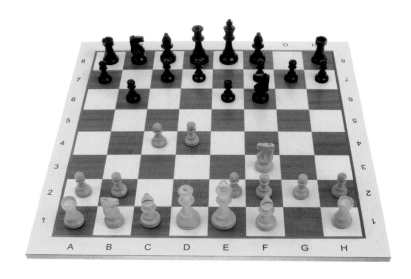

Here is a typical position in the Queen's Indian Defense. Black has completed a Queenside fianchetto and is ready to castle. However, with black to move, black has the option of preventing e3-e4 by playing Nf6-e4. This sharp resource is one of reasons this defense is popular.

CONTINUED ON NEXT PAGE

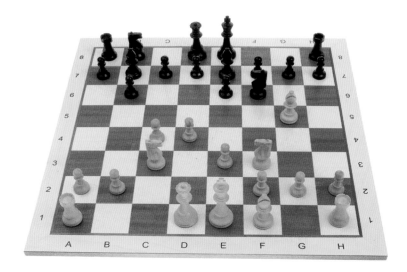

The Nimzo-Indian Defense (1.d2-d4 Ng8-f6 2.c2-c4 e7-e6 3.Nb1-c3 Bf8-b4)

The very popular *Nimzo-Indian Defense* is named after Aron Nimzovitch, a great chess theorist of the early 20th century. In this opening, black aggressively prevents white from playing e2-e4 by pinning the white Knight on c3.

As you can see, white has developed normally with 2.c2-c4 and with 3.Nb1-c3. Black has responded with 1.Ng8-f6, 2.e7-e6, and, unlike the Queen's Indian, with 3.Bf8-b4. The Bishop on b4 pins the white Knight on c3 and, by so doing, prevents white from playing 4.e2-e4. If white were to play 4.e2-e4, black would simply capture the e4-pawn with the Knight on f6 (Nf6).

As you might expect, the early placement of the black Bishop on b4 can lead to its exchange for the white Knight on c3. Often, the white c-pawns become doubled, but white will then have an uncontested dark-squared Bishop as compensation.

FAQ

Why do we call these Indian Defenses?

The term *Indian Defense* comes from the ancient chess-like game chaturanga. Chaturanga originated in India circa 7th century. A common opening move in this game was to develop a Bishop on the wing—we call this a fianchetto today. For more on fianchettos, see Chapter 5, "Bishop Strategy."

If you're careful about fighting for the center and guarding your material, you're likely to avoid a catastrophe in the opening. As you might expect, there are many bad openings. There are even a number of chess books dedicated to the study of such moves. Here are two bad openings, the *Englund Gambit* and the *Spike*. They have glamorous names, but make no mistake: These are openings to avoid.

THE ENGLUND GAMBIT (1.D2-D4 E7-E5?)

In this opening, black responds to white's 1.d2-d4 with an awful move that simply loses a pawn. As you can see, the *Englund Gambit* involves an immediate 1.e7-e5 by black. On just the second move, white wins a pawn with little or no compensation for black. To win the pawn, of course, white simply plays 2.d4xe5.

THE SPIKE

The name of this opening is far more compelling than the move itself. Rather than contest the center, white opens the game with 1.g2-g4. Black should respond to white's flank move by capturing a part of the center with 1.d7-d5 or 1.e7-e5.

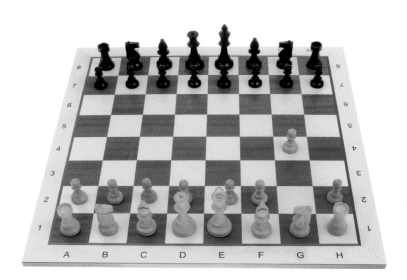

chapter 10

Common Opening Formations

To improve in chess, it helps to be able to recognize certain pawn structures and have a coordinated plan for how to proceed. In this chapter, I present several different structures and opening formations. Most are relatively easy to set up and can be very effective even in the hands of a relatively inexperienced player. As you will see, every structure has its strengths and weaknesses. Understanding the role of each piece within the structure will help guide your play.

The first two sections involve opening formations that you might use with the white pieces. The second two are structures commonly used by the player with the black pieces. The only danger is that you might decide to set up these formations without regard to what your opponent is doing. It's great to have these plans at your disposal, but watch and consider all of your opponent's moves before you play your next move.

King's Indian Attack

Unlike most of the openings presented in Chapter 9, the King's Indian Attack is a very patient opening system that seeks to develop all of white's pieces before initiating any attack. You might not win with it, but at least no one will be able to run you off the board quickly.

The King's Indian Attack is essentially a King's Indian Defense, but played with the white pieces rather than with black. As you might expect, the extra move that white has by moving first gives the opening a bit more punch than the defense.

In the King's Indian Attack, white aims to achieve this position by move 7. Note that white has fianchettoed the light-squared Bishop. The Knight on g1 has developed to f3. The Knight on b1 has developed to d2. White has a modest but solid central pawn structure with pawns on d3 and e4.

To achieve this position, white could have opened the game with either 1.e2-e4 or even 1.Ng1-f3. Many players reach this position by playing 1.Ng1-f3 first, fiancettoing quickly with 2.g2-g3 and 3.Bf1-g2, and then castling. It may surprise you that the move e2-e4 can actually be played in this opening system on move 7 rather than on move 1. So, after castling, white might continue with 5.d2-d3, 6.Nb1-d2, and finally 7.e2-e4.

White's next moves very much depend, of course, on what black is trying to do. But white does have a straightforward plan for making progress. As long as the Knight can't be captured there, white might try Nf3-h4, or otherwise Nf3-e1, followed by the quick advance of the f-pawn from f2-f4.

In this position, white is getting ready to attack with e4-e5 or possibly f4-f5. Perhaps you might decide first to develop the Queen to e2 or (after the Nd2 moves) Bc1-e3. However you proceed, you have the possibility to play ten moves or so without significant error, even against a relatively strong player. Even if you lose eventually, your opponent will be impressed that you have made quick progress as a chess player, and you will have the opportunity for an exciting middlegame with an active set of pieces. For middlegame strategies, see Chapter 11.

This King's Indian Attack position was reached after just seven moves. White has reached the ideal position. Black responded to 7.e2-e4 by pushing the d-pawn through to d4. In this position, white decides to play Nd2-c4, an interesting move that combines with the Nf3 to attack the black e5-pawn twice. Black is forced to defend the pawn by playing 8.Qd8-c7.

CONTINUED ON NEXT PAGE

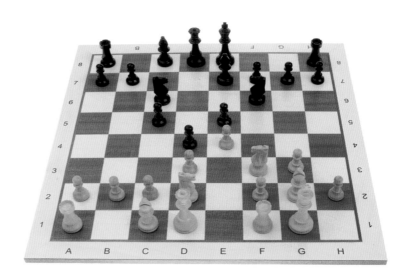

Rather than play quickly or automatically, white realizes that black might try to attack the Nc4 by playing b7-b5. White would like to keep the Knight on c4, near the middle of the board. White therefore plays 9.a2-a4 in order to safeguard the Nc4 from attack. Notice that the Nd2-c4 maneuver now permits Bc1 to move out, perhaps to the g5 square. If you find this kind of position to your liking, you now know how to reach it!

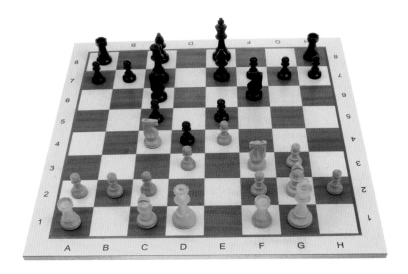

FAQ

What is correspondence chess?

In this age of the Internet, it may be hard to believe that proponents of playing chess through the mail still exist. Correspondence chess, also known as postal chess, is perhaps the slowest form of chess, with international games lasting as long as 3 to 4 years! Postal chess players enjoy taking days over each move, exploring all the possibilities. But in the age of chess software, e-mail, and chess websites, correspondence chess could be on its way out.

To get started in postal chess, try one of the dedicated postal chess organizations. The U.S. Chess Federation (www.uschess.org/cc/) runs its own postal tournaments. The International Correspondence Chess Federation (www.iccf.com) organizes international events.

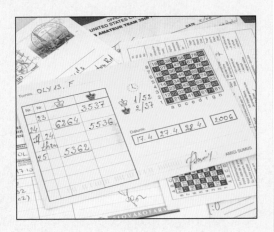

The Colle System carries the name of the Belgian master, Edgard Colle, who used it to win many brilliant games in the 1920s. The Colle System is very much like the Slav Defense but is played with the white pieces rather than with black.

White begins the game with a rather unassuming setup. Rather than fight immediately for the center, white has chosen a pawn structure that delays the occupation of e4. This idea is very simple. White wants to prepare e3-e4 rather than play it immediately. And so note that the white Qc2, the Bd3, the Nd2, and the Re1 are all poised to support the move e3-e4. When the move comes, it will have half an army to defend it.

To bring the position about, white usually begins the game with 1.d2-d4, and continues with 2.Ng1-f3, 3.e2-e3, 4.Nb1-d2 (Knights before Bishops), and then 5.c2-c3, 6.Bf1-d3, and then castles Kingside (0-0), Rf1-e1, and Qd1-c2. Be sure not to play these moves automatically. If black initiates a capture, be sure to recapture. And do not permit black to safely advance the black e-pawn to e4 where it would fork white's Bd3 and Nf3.

In this position from a real game, white plays 9.e3-e4 immediately in order to threaten e4-e5, forking the Bd6 and the Nf6. As you can see, the e4-push can be very strong, and white will usually develop a strong attack if the pawn can safely advance to the e5-square.

If there is a drawback to the Colle System, it is that white has made no effort to activate the Bc1. With black, you should certainly try to prevent white from playing e3-e4 and, if possible, to advance the black e-pawn to the key e4-square.

Hedgehog

Just as the Colle System and the King's Indian Attack are all-purpose attacks for white, the Hedgehog is an all-purpose defense for black. It's not a gimmick or a second-rate defense. I used it to win the 10th U.S. Correspondence Chess Championship, and some of the strongest players in the world continue to make it their main weapon. The Hedgehog is an animal akin to the porcupine: Get too close and you will get poked.

Here is the Hedgehog pawn structure. The black pawns on a6, b6, d6, and e6 form a defensive wall that aims to prevent white from advancing. Some people believe that the black pawn structure resembles a hedgehog, hence its name. Note that the black c-pawn is missing. Black usually exchanges the c-pawn for the white d-pawn, as you have already seen in the Sicilian Defense.

This example illustrates a common setup for all of black's pieces within the Hedgehog. Note that the black Rooks are aggressively doubled on the c-file. The Bishop on b7 and the Queen on a8 are joining forces with the Nf6 to deliver three attacks on the white e4-pawn. The Knight on d7 can help direct the attack. If the Knight moves to e5, it will become the third attack on the white c-pawn. If the Nd7 moves to c5, it will become the fourth attack on white's e4-pawn.

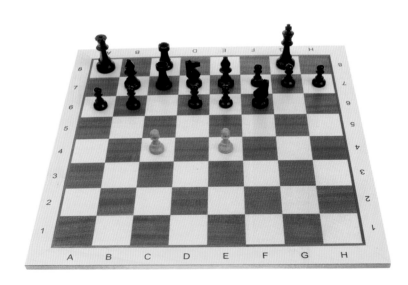

One of the best features of the Hedgehog is that there are no meaningful pawn weaknesses in the black camp. To reach the Hedgehog structure, black can play a Sicilian against 1.e2-e4. When white plays d2-d4, black should capture the pawn so long as a Knight or a Queen will recapture. Black usually begins to set up the Hedgehog structure with e7-e6, a7-a6, d7-d6, Ng8-f6, Nb8-d7, and often Qd8-c7. The Bishops then move to e7 and b7 and, after castling, black will play Ra8-c8. The Queen on c7 "tucks" to b8 and perhaps to a8, where it is very safe from attack, and plays an important role in attacking the white center.

The Hedgehog is considered an all-purpose weapon because it can be reached easily against 1.e2-e4, 1.c2-c4, and 1.Ng1-f3, all by beginning with black's move 1.c7-c5.

This position illustrates a common Hedgehog tactic. Black has completed the development of all the pieces. Black now plays b6-b5, knowing that if white captures on b5 with the c4-pawn, black can unleash the power of the doubled Rooks with Rook capturing Nc3.

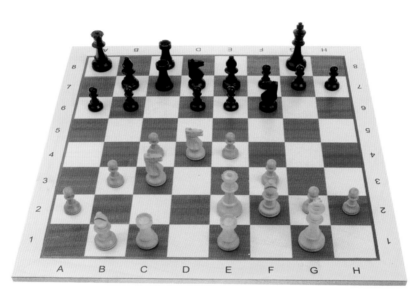

Avant-Garde

The Avant-Garde, as its name may imply, is a modern attempt to create a truly all-purpose approach for black. In this opening structure, white develops all of the Knights and Bishops fairly quickly, but in a very distinct way. Many players will not be happy with its cramped approach to the game but, like the other systems we've examined, it has the merit of keeping even a beginner in the game against a much stronger opponent.

You will see that this setup would not be difficult to achieve. Both Bishops are fianchettoed, the Knights have developed toward the center at d7 and e7. Black's position is cramped but quite versatile; there are no weaknesses. Most white players decide to expand in the center and simply can't resist trying to break down this system.

In this figure showing black's position as well as a portion of white's center, white can decide to move forward with e4-e5. Black will not capture on e5 but rather will respond with d6-d5 and then c7-c5, counterattacking on the Queenside.

If, instead, white attacks with d4-d5, black, rather than capture, will often play e6-e5 and then f7-f5, counterattacking on the Kingside. One Canadian Grandmaster, Duncan Suttles, made a chess career out of playing such positions with black and with white as well. Many others find the system to be very slow, but Suttles showed that with sufficient patience, the Avant-Garde can be a dangerous weapon.

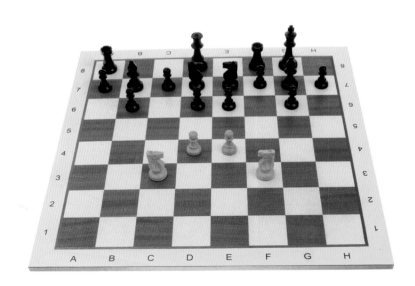

Just as the Hedgehog pawn structure does not look much like a hedgehog, the Dragon structure doesn't really look like a dragon. "Dragon" describes the Kingside pawns that are said to be the dragon's head, and the Queenside pawns that form its tail.

The Dragon is a specific variation of the Sicilian Defense, but for our purposes, think of the Dragon simply as one possible strategy for developing the white and black pieces. In this position, black has fianchettoed the dark-squared Bishop within the Dragon's head and castled on the Kingside. Black's formation is set for a sharp attack on the white Queenside.

Black's decision is whether to attack first with the pawns or with the pieces. In a pawn-led attack, black might advance the a-pawn to a6 and the b-pawn to b5 and then perhaps on to b4. Then black might continue with Qd8–a5. In a piece-led attack, black might play Bc8-d7 and Ra8-c8, bringing the Rook quickly to the open c-file. Black might then continue with Nc6-e5 and then Ne5-c4, where the Knight would fork the white Queen and the Bishop on e3.

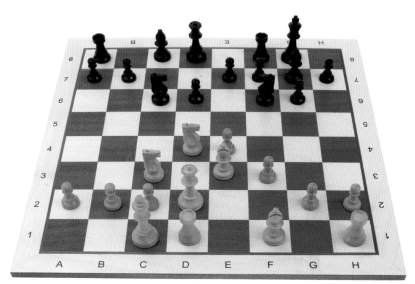

The position is "double-edged" because white also has a plan to slay the Dragon. White has two ideas here. The pawn-led attack involves g2-g4 and then h2-h4-h5, an effort to pry open the h-file for the Rook on h1 and perhaps also the Queen after Qd2-h2.

In a piece-led attack, white might try Bf1-c4 as well as Be3-h6—an attempt to exchange black's dark-squared Bishop, which is an important defender of the black Kingside. In order to fianchetto, black had to advance the g-pawn to g6. We know that every pawn move creates weaknesses. In this case, the h6-square is no longer defended by the black g-pawn.

Notice how carefully white has constructed the attack to go after the weakness on h6. White has castled on the Queenside in order to be able to push the Kingside pawns forward without compromising the King's safety. And white has pointed the Qd2 and the Be3 toward the key h6-square. White has also safeguarded the Be3 by placing the f-pawn on f3 where it prevents the annoying Nf6-g4.

CONTINUED ON NEXT PAGE

During tournament play in this position, white (Anatoly Karpov) and black (Victor Kortchnoi) were engaged in a titanic struggle in which white eventually won. In this Dragon, white has succeeded in exchanging the dark-squared Bishops and, hoping to play Qh6xh7, would now like to eliminate the key Nf6. Karpov therefore played g4-g5 and, after black's Rc5xg5, continued with the amazing Rd3-d5, a move that looks bad because the Nf6 attacks the d5-square. Of course, the Nf6 must not move because it is needed to defend the h7-square from the threat of Qh6xh7. As you can appreciate, games in the Dragon tend to be among the most complex in chess.

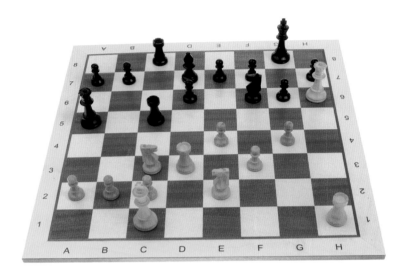

TIP

If playing the game is the best way to improve, reading chess books is a close second. There are thousands of books about chess out there. Some even focus solely on openings.

However, I recommend that beginners shy away from the chess opening books. Instead, stick with ones that focus on *complete* games—openings, middlegames, and endgames.

Many of my students have enjoyed Irving Chernev's classic *Logical Chess Move by Move.* To sharpen your tactics, try Fred Reinfeld's *1001 Brilliant Ways to Checkmate.* As you progress, I hope that you also discover two special chess classics: Bobby Fischer's *My 60 Memorable Games* and David Bronstein's *Zurich, 1953.*

The truth is, you will benefit from any chess book, as long as you spend time with it and give thought to the various positions. Reading about chess is a surefire way to improve.

Named after Simon Winawer, the French Winawer was popularized by Aron Nimzovitch and later by World Champion Mikael Botvinnik. A variation of the French Defense, it provides another instructive pawn structure.

As you saw in Chapter 9, in the French Defense, white is able to place both the d- and e-pawns on the 4th rank. Black supports the d7-d5 counter with e7-e6. The French Winawer variation begins after 3.Nb1-c3 and then black's move, 3.Bf8-b4. This Bishop move is interesting. Black breaks the rule of moving a Bishop before a Knight, but the pin on white's Nc3 is annoying. The Knight was defending the white e4-pawn, which white must now advance or further defend.

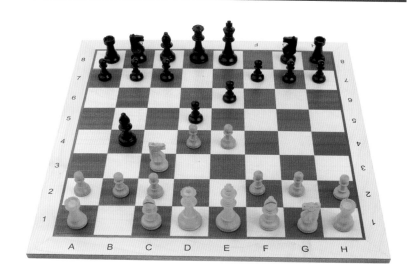

White prefers to push with 4.e4-e5 in order to imprison black's bad light-squared Bishop on c8. The pawn chain that emerges has the strong pawn on e5 but also the weak pawn on d4. Black therefore plays the move 4.c7-c5 in an effort to disrupt white's pawn chain. White now "puts the question" to the black Bb4 with 5.a2-a3. After all, the Bishop moved early and is now being forced to move again.

CONTINUED ON NEXT PAGE

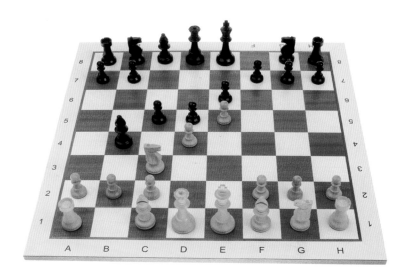

Black responds by capturing the Nc3 with Bb4, check, and white of course recaptures with the b2-pawn. The following position includes one additional move by black, 6.Ng8-e7, a logical square for the Knight now that the white pawn on e5 is guarding the natural f6-square.

In this interesting position, notice that both sides have long pawn chains. White's pawn chain stretches from c3 through e5, while black's reaches from the backward pawn on f7 through to d5. As a result of the two chains, black's Bishop on c8 is bad because it is boxed in by the fixed black pawns. Unfortunately for black, the good dark-squared Bishop has already been traded.

White can try to take advantage of the absence of black's dark-squared Bishop in two ways. First, white could advance the a-pawn once again to a4 and then play Bc1-a3. From a3, the Bishop would exert powerful pressure on the a3-f8 diagonal.

Or, white could play the surprising Qd1-g4. White has not yet developed the Ng1 or the Bishops, but the early Queen move causes a real problem for black. With the black Bishop gone from f8, how should black defend the pawn on g7? Black could castle, but it's not hard to visualize a powerful attack brewing with moves such as Bf1-d3, Bc1-h6, h2-h4, Rh1-h3-g3, and Ng1-e2-f4.

In response to 7.Qd1-g4, black could push the g-pawn to g6. But every pawn move creates weaknesses, in this case on the f6 and h6 squares. In most games, black therefore plays 7.Qd8–c7, permitting white to capture the g7-pawn and hoping for counter-play on the Queenside.

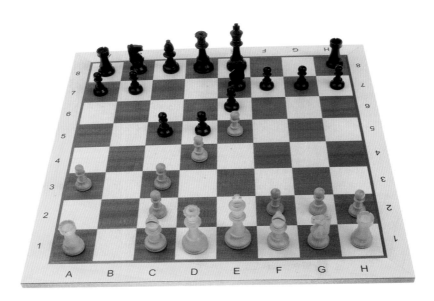

Like an old stone wall in New England, the Stonewall's pawn formation is set in stone. In this pawn structure, no attack will proceed through the center. If either player attempts to push their e-pawn, it will be lost. The attacks will therefore occur on the flanks.

Notice that each side will have a bad Bishop. This fixed structure makes white's dark-squared Bishop bad. Black's light-squared Bishop will also be bad. Each side would very much like to trade its bad Bishop for another Bishop or a Knight.

In open positions, Bishops are better than Knights. Here, with the pawns locked in the center, the Knights can be more valuable. This is a stonewall position in which black is doing very well. Black has managed to trade the light-squared Bishop for a Knight on the f3-square. Black's Knight on e4 is especially strong, located in the middle of the board where the enemy pawns can't attack it.

White would also like to place a Knight on the key e5-square, but the Queen on f3, which arrived there to recapture black's Bishop, is blocking the Nd2's path to f3 and then e5. With such wonderful activity, black draws up a neat attacking plan. Black will play Kg8-h8, slide the Rf8-g8, and attempt to attack on the flank with g7-g5.

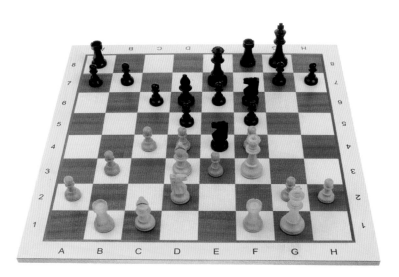

Benoni

The Benoni is an interesting defense against 1.d2-d4 that creates an imbalanced pawn structure that often results in very spirited games that aggressive players tend to appreciate. Black begins the game like the Indian Defenses in Chapter 9 with 1.Ng8-f6 and, after white's 2.c2-c4, black continues with 2.c7-c5. The Benoni formation was named for a biblical reference. Benoni means, literally, "son of sorrow." A forte for a time of World Champion Alexander Alekhine, it is a frequent visitor in tournament play.

As you can see in this position, the black pawn on c5 presents three options to white. White can capture the black c5-pawn, but that would simply double white's c-pawns and invite black to recapture in any number of ways. The strongest method for black would probably be 3.e7-e6, hoping to recapture with the Bishop. If then 4.b2-b4, black has the strong response 4.a7-a5, attacking the b4-c5 pawn chain at the base.

As an alternative, white could defend the pawn with Ng1-f3, but that would invite black to capture the d4-pawn with the flank c5-pawn and reach a Hedgehog position with e7-e6, a7-a6, and Qd8-c7.

White's best move in this position is to push the d4-pawn to d5. Here is the position after 3.d4-d5 e7-e6, 4.Nb1-c3 e6xd5, 5.c4xd5 d7-d6. As you can see, there is a significant imbalance in the pawn structure. Black has three pawns on the Queenside, a majority compared to white's two pawns. By contrast, white has a five-on-four advantage on the Kingside.

White would like to continue with e2-e4 with the idea of preparing for an e4-e5 advance. Apart from trying to prevent white's advance of the e-pawn, black will try to advance the Queenside pawns. The fianchetto of the black's dark-squared Bishop and castling on the Kingside will assist in that goal.

Here is a Benoni after 12 moves. Black has fianchettoed the dark-squared Bishop, castled, and brought a Rook to e8 to watch over the key e5-square. Black has also prepared to advance the b7-pawn by playing the Nb8-a6-c7 and by sliding the Rook from a8 to b8.

White played f2-f4 to support an e4-e5 advance. The Be2 is likely soon to support the white center with Be2-f3. The Nd2 will likely move to c4 in order to support e4-e5 and to place some pressure on black's weak pawn on d6.

TIP

Practice with Online Chess

A good place to practice opening formations is online. There are many places to play chess on the Internet these days. Many are free; a few charge a modest fee.

If you just want to play a light game of chess at any hour, try one of these websites:

- Yahoo: games.yahoo.com
- Pogo: www.pogo.com
- MSN: http://zone.msn.com/en/chess/default.htm
- www.chessclub.com
- www.playchess.com

Middlegame Strategy

Many players memorize long opening variations but have little or no idea how to proceed once they get to the middle of a game. You already know about having good and bad pieces, placing Rooks on open files, placing the Knights in the center where the enemy pawns can't attack them, and trying to avoid bad Bishops. In this chapter, I offer four basic principles and strategies that will help you integrate many of these ideas.

Aron Nimzovitsch, a great German Grandmaster of the early 20th century, introduced new ways of thinking about chess. His chess classic, *My System,* is a long and complex book that was awkwardly translated to English. In the first section, I introduce his five steps to victory in an easy-to-understand manner.

In the second section, I introduce two important ways of approaching your thought process in every chess game. The first, the idea of selecting and considering options, at least three "candidate moves," was popularized in Alexander's Kotov's 1971 classic *Think Like a Grandmaster.* The idea is simple enough. In every position, consider not one move but at least three. Or, as the great player Emanuel Lasker put it, "When you see a good move, look for a better one."

In the third section, I offer an important way of thinking about "threats." Before every move, consider whether your opponent is threatening to do something important. In response, you must either turn off the threat or else find a threat that is more significant. And finally, in the fourth section, I emphasize the importance of recapturing after someone captures one of your pieces.

Five Steps to Victory

The five steps that I outline here were first discussed by Grandmaster Aron Nimzovitsch in his books *My System* and *Blockade*. He never actually called them "the five steps to victory," but these steps are discussed extensively in his books. The five steps are relatively simple but account for many of my victories, and they are present in one form or another in many, if not most, master games.

The Steps

STEP 1: IDENTIFY THE WEAKNESS

The first step is simple enough. You will win many games if you train yourself to be aware of and to quickly identify all of your opponent's pawn weaknesses. In this example, the two central black pawns on d6 and e5 form a pawn chain. As you saw in Chapter 6, "Pawn Strategy," the backward pawn at d6 is the weaker of the two pawns because no pawn can defend it. Black's d6-pawn represents a key weakness in the black pawn structure. Having identified the key weakness on d6, you are ready for step 2.

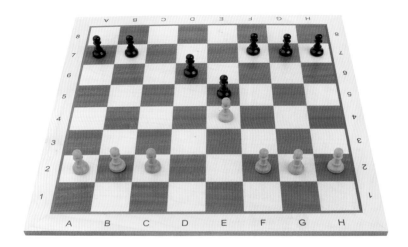

STEP 2: FIX THE WEAKNESS

The second step is quite simple. To prevent black from pushing the d6-pawn to d5, white must fix black's weakness by occupying or controlling the d5-square.

In Chapter 4, "Knight Strategy," you learned that it is advantageous to place Knights in the center of the board where they can't be attacked by pawns. Here, you can see that it would be helpful to place a Knight—or another piece, for that matter—in the "hole" at d5.

By moving the Knight to d5, or even by using the Knight to control d5, you will prevent black from eliminating the d6-pawn weakness by pushing the pawn from d6 to d5. In this figure, white controls the key d5-square with both the Knight on e3 and the pawn on e4. If black were to push the d6-pawn to d5, white would be able to win it. With the Knight on e3, the pawn on d6 has been fixed because it can't successfully move without being lost.

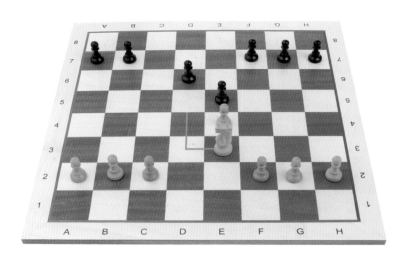

STEP 3: ATTACK THE WEAKNESS WITH YOUR PIECES

Once you have identified and fixed the weakness, it's time for step 3: Attack the weakness with your pieces—not your pawns. In this position, it is clear that white has successfully arranged an attack on black's d6-pawn with four different pieces, the doubled Rooks on d2 and d3, the Queen on d1, and even the dark-squared Bishop on a3. Notice that white's attack has been patient in that the Queen is not leading the charge on d3 but rather is attacking from the rear on d1. Strong players know that it's often more effective to have the less valuable pieces lead the attack. As they say in boxing, "Don't lead with your nose."

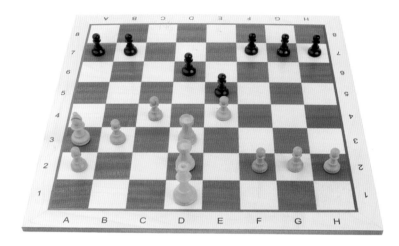

STEP 4: YOUR OPPONENT WILL BE FORCED TO DEFEND THE WEAKNESS

If you have successfully carried out the first three steps, your opponent must carry out step 4. For every one of your attacks on the pawn weakness, your opponent will have to find a defender. If your opponent fails to defend the pawn adequately, look to take the target-pawn first "with the little thing." What "little thing," you ask? It depends on the position but it is often a Knight or a Bishop.

In this position, white is still attacking black's d6-pawn with four pieces, and black has responded by defending the poor d6-pawn with four pieces—Rd8, Rd7, Be7, and Qb8. As a result, these pieces aren't very active.

Note that, as a result of the first four steps, white has two active Rooks on a semi-open file, while black's Rooks are stuck defending the d6-pawn. White has a good Bishop on a3, attacking the d6-pawn, while black's Be7 is bad, stuck behind the fixed d6-pawn. Even the white Queen on d1 is more active than its black counterpart on b8.

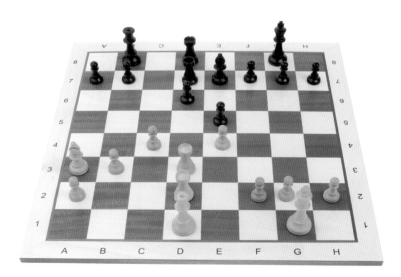

CONTINUED ON NEXT PAGE

STEP 5: ATTACK THE WEAKNESS WITH A PAWN

By the time your opponent has completed step 4, he'll know that there's trouble ahead. Most or all of your pieces will be active by focusing their energy on a single fixed point. By contrast, your opponent's pieces will be relatively weak, defending rather than attacking a weakness.

For the final step, attack the weakness with a pawn. As you can see in this position, white has simply advanced the c4-pawn to c5 and black is in a quandary. The black d6-pawn has three options. It can capture on c5, push forward to d5, or remain where it is. We know that the pawn can't push forward to d5 because it is fixed. On d5, white would have four attacks on the pawn while black would have only two defenses (the Rooks).

Instead, if black were to capture with d6xc5, white would suddenly have three attacks on the Rd7. Capturing the white pawn would lose a black Rook.

Black could do nothing, but white would still have five attacks on the d6-pawn, and black would have only four defenses. On white's next move, white would continue with c5xd6, winning the key black pawn.

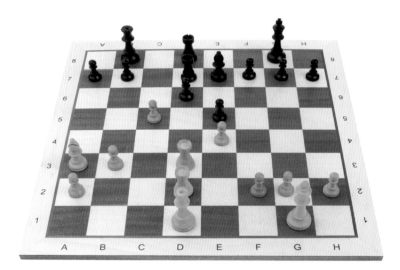

TIP

See the Five Steps to Victory in Action Online!
Observing other players online is a great way to learn and to see the five steps in action. PlayChess (www.playchess.com) and Internet Chess Club (www.chessclub.com) are pay-sites that offer fairly competitive games, but you can log in as a guest and watch live grandmaster events from all over the world.

PlayChess is my personal favorite, and you will often find me playing there with the login name jedwards.

The Five Steps in Practice

In this position, with black to move, black realizes that the white b3-pawn is a weakness and is already fixed by the black c5-pawn and the black Nc6. Black plays Nc6-a7, threatening to capture Bb5 and, by forcing the Bishop to move, gaining access for Rb8-b4. White responds with Bb5-e2.

Black continues with the strategy by playing Rb8-b4, helping to fix the pawn and preparing to bring the Rc8 into the strategy by doubling the Rooks on the b-file. Understanding black's strategy, white attempts to bring the King closer to the b-pawn by playing Kf1-e1.

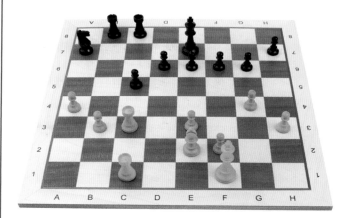

Black continues with Rc8-b8, placing a second attack on the white b3-pawn. For the moment, white has only one defender, the Rc3. White therefore plays Be2-d1, using the Bishop to defend b3. There are now two attacks and two defenses. The third attack will require that the black Knight reach the a5-square.

Black plays Na7-c6. Knowing there will soon be a third attack, white could defend again with Rc1-b1, but Rb1 would be vulnerable after Rb4xa4 because the b3-pawn would be pinned and unable to recapture on a4 without losing Rb1. White therefore plays Rc1-a1 with the idea of defending the b3-pawn with a Rook on a3.

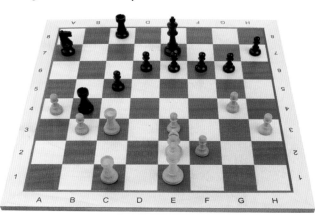

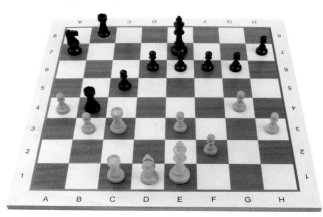

CONTINUED ON NEXT PAGE

Black now continues with Nc6-a5, placing the b3-pawn under a third attack. White has no choice but to defend the pawn with its Rook and plays Ra1-a3.

The only step remaining is to attack b3 with the c5-pawn (c5-c4). Black, in no rush, delayed for a moment to fix another one of the white pawns on a dark square with g6-g5. White responded with a bad move, Ke1-d2, permitting the black Knight to move later toward the center with a powerful check (Na5-c4+).

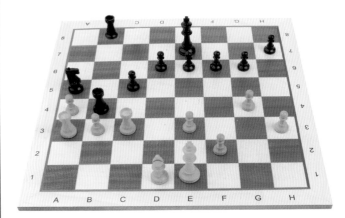

Finally, the fifth step. Black plays c5-c4, making the fourth attack on the white b-pawn. A pawn capture on c4 not only weakens the white pawn structure, but also permits Na5xc4+: a Knight fork that attacks white's Kd2 and Ra3. If white does nothing, black will be able to capture and win the b3-pawn.

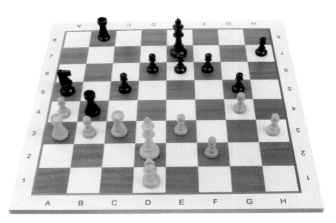

TIP

Practice with Chess Software

Chess software and websites are transforming how to play chess. Anyone with a computer can play against software that can challenge even the best players in the world.

Most of the current chess software programs are so strong that many players can get discouraged quickly. No human enjoys losing game after game, but the advantage is clear: You have a built-in opponent who is happy to play at any hour of the day or night.

Keep in mind that the engines in the software are simply number-crunching and never tire. They play a very different game than humans do, and as long as you keep that in mind, you can use them to hone your skills. The engines almost always permit you to take back a bad move—a nice advantage when you're learning.

Consider your options (candidates) at every move. Very few masters move quickly. Instead, they tend to play very thoughtfully. But what are they thinking about?

At every move, most strong players consider at least three different moves. That may surprise beginners, who are content to play the first good-looking move they find. Emmanuel Lasker summed it up by explaining that even after you find a strong move, keep looking. You may find something stronger.

Making Plans

Many beginners believe that the masters have trained themselves to think many moves ahead. The fact is that masters have an advantage. Masters rarely calculate long forced sequences. Although some rely on intuition or an innate feel for the game, most are able to plan ahead. They have a sense of where the strongest squares are and where each piece belongs. From experience, they know how to conduct attacks and how to coordinate their pieces.

To illustrate the process, this section follows the ideas and considerations through 12 consecutive moves of a master game.

In this first position, white already has a tangible advantage. The move Nf3-g5 has already caused black to prevent Bd3xh7 with the move g7-g6, a pawn advance that has weakened the black Kingside. Notice that by moving the g-pawn forward, the f6 and h6 squares are now weak. White would like to move the dark-squared Bishop on c1 to h6 where it would attack the black Rf8 and also control the g7-square in front of the black King. White would also like to further weaken the black Kingside.

White therefore has two ideas. The first is the move Qf3-h3 with the threat of Qh3xh7 checkmate (Ng5 would defend Qh7). The threat of checkmate would require black to weaken the Kingside with h7-h5. White could also try Ng5-e4, which is a strong looking move with the idea of both Ne4-f6 check as well as opening the Bc1's path to the h6 square.

Both plans are legitimate. Although you should keep in mind the principle that when two moves look good, one is always better than the other. In this case, white plays Qf3-h3 in order to further weaken the black Kingside.

CONTINUED ON NEXT PAGE

As you can see, black has prevented the immediate checkmate by advancing the h7-pawn to h5, but the pawn move has further weakened the black Kingside. It would now be more difficult, for example, to drive the Ng5 away, and the support for the g6-pawn has been reduced.

White might again try Ng5-e4 with the idea of Ne4-f6 check and Bc1-h6. That idea seems even stronger now that the Kingside is weaker. White could also try to advance the f-pawn to f4 and then f5. Or white could play g2-g4 to try to batter down the black Kingside.

White must decide whether to conduct a pawn-led or a piece-led attack. Both pawn moves weaken the white Kingside. White therefore decides on the first course of action, Ng5-e4, with the idea of activating the Bc1. Black responds by capturing on d5 with the Ne7. The Nd5 will be well posted in the center of the board where the white pawns will not be able to attack it.

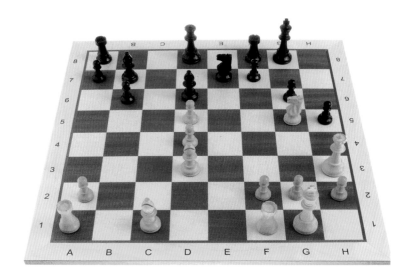

White has three candidate moves in this next position. White could capture the Bd6 with the Ne4. White could develop the Bc1 directly to h6, or white could play Bc1-g5. Both Bishop moves take advantage of the weak dark squares around the King.

White's move Ne4xBd6 is very tempting because, in the open board, the Bishop has considerable sway. However, the Knight is a powerful piece in the center of the board where, to drive it away, black would have to play f7-f5, further weakening black's Kingside.

The most tempting move is white's Bc1-h6, but white would lose quickly after this move with black's Bb7-c8 attacking the white Queen. In that position, the Queen would be quickly trapped in the center of the board after Qh3-f3 and Bc8-g4.

Having seen the trap, white avoids it by first playing the move Bc1-g5, attacking the black Queen. To guard the Queen, black responds with Bd6-e7.

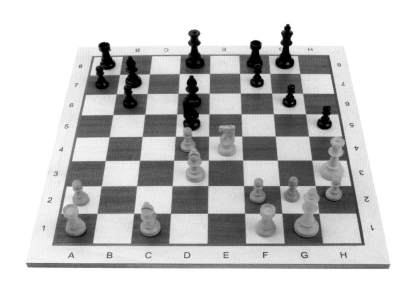

After black's Bd6-e7, black is threatening simply to capture the white Bg5. White therefore has two options: capture the black Be7 or play the move Bg5-h6. Fortunately, after Bg5-h6, black is no longer able to trap the white Queen because, without the black Bishop on d6, the Queen will have access to the g3-square. Rather than exchange Bishops, which would reduce the firepower aimed at the black King, white plays Bg5-h6. This move, of course, attacks the Rf8. Rather than move the Rook, black plays Bb7-c8, attacking the white Queen.

With the attack by the Bc8 on the Qh3, white has two logical moves. To save the Qh3, white can move it to f3 or to g3. On f3, the Queen would be subject to another attack with Bc8-g4. White therefore decides to play Qg3 where the Queen, in conjunction with the Bd3, is generating pressure on the weakened g6-pawn. Black responds by moving Rf8-e8, out of danger from the attack from the Bh6.

CONTINUED ON NEXT PAGE

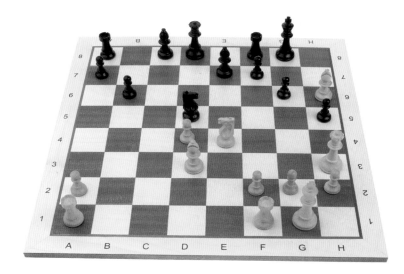

White has many good moves in this position. For example, white could activate the Ra1 to c1 or the Rf1-e1. The Bd3 could move to b5 to attack the Re8. Or white could play Qg3-e5, threatening checkmate in one move with Qe5-g7. Both Rook moves look useful, but masters know that Rook moves are often the most difficult moves to make because it is hard to know exactly where the Rooks belong. White decides to play Qg3-e5, in part because the move is very difficult to meet. After Qg3-e5 black can't respond with Be7-f6. White would then play the amazing Qe5xNd5, seeing that after black's Qd8xd5, white plays Ne4xBf6 check, forking the King, the e8-Rook, and the black Queen on d5.

Black therefore must block the checkmate by white's Queen on g7 by advancing the f7-pawn to f6, yet another weakening of the black Kingside. In this case, the f7-f6 move weakens the now undefended g6-pawn.

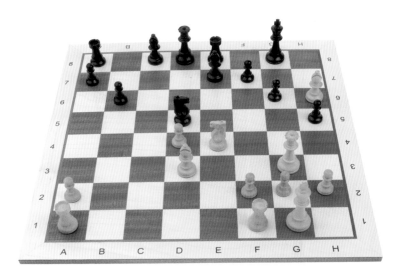

Having forced yet another Kingside weakness, the white Queen must now retreat. In this instance, there is only one safe move: Qe5-g3. Fortunately for white, the Qg3 will now attack the black g6-pawn. To defend it, black decides to push the g6-pawn to g5.

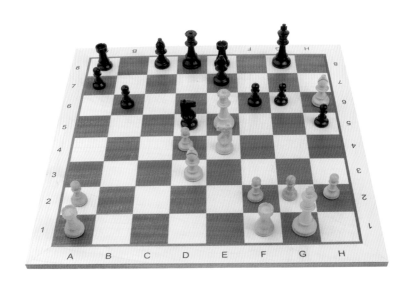

White's strategy has worked very well. As a result of carefully timed maneuvers, black's Kingside is in shambles. However, black does suddenly emerge with the idea of trapping the Bh6 behind enemy lines. White could develop one of its Rooks, but to take advantage of the Bh6's advanced position, white decides to play h2-h4. Note that the pawn on h4 represents the fourth attack on the black g5-pawn. Under such pressure, black has no choice but to push the g-pawn yet again.

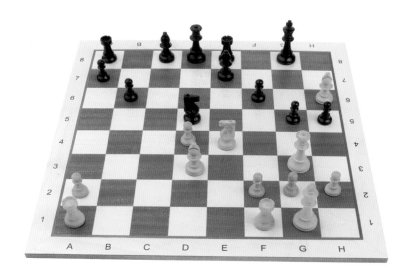

This position represents the culmination of white's initial strategy of forcing the black Kingside pawns to advance. Having caused the damage, white now considers the next phase: how best to take advantage of the open diagonals and the entry squares around the black King.

White has many interesting options and, as many strong players like to say, even a bad plan is better than no plan. White could now take aim on the a2-g8 diagonal with moves such as Bd3-c4 and Qg3-b3. Alternatively, white could begin with Ra1-c1 or Rf1-e1. Another interesting option is Ra1-e1, with the idea of advancing the f-pawn against black's weak pawn structure.

White decides on the first plan of Bd3-c4, putting pressure on the white center, pinning the black Nd5 against the Kg8, and taking aim on the e6 and f7 squares. Black responds, as masters often do, by moving the King in order to break the pin (Kg8-h7).

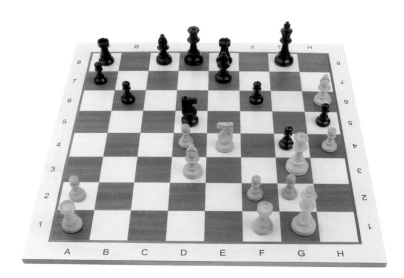

CONTINUED ON NEXT PAGE

In this position, white faces the need to retreat the Bh6. Retreating the Bishop to g5 would lose the Bishop to the f6-pawn. Retreating back to c1 makes little sense, because the Ra1 will probably want to develop there. That leaves d2, e3, and f4. The e3-square is relatively inactive because of the fixed d4-pawn, and, with a Bishop on e3, the Qg3 would be blocked from the b3 square. White decides to retreat the Bishop to d2 where, three squares away from the centralized black Nd5, the Bishop dominates the black Knight. Fearful of white's activity and mindful of the Kingside weaknesses, black responds with Bc8-f5, attacking the undefended Ne4 and immediately taking control over the b1-h7 diagonal on which the black King is sitting.

With no reasonable retreat for the white Ne4, white will need to defend it. Qg3-d3 is unacceptable because white would not want to walk into a pin. Retreating the Bc4-d3 blocks the Queen's access to the b3 square and the Bc4's real idea is to pressure the a2-g8 diagonal. White therefore needs to choose between Ra1-e1 or Rf1-e1. Ra1-e1 would probably commit white to using the Rf1 to push the f-pawn. Rf1-e1 would give white the opportunity to use the Ra1 on the c-file.

White selects Rf1-e1 as the more flexible move. Black responds with Bf5-g6 in an effort to fight for control over the f7-square.

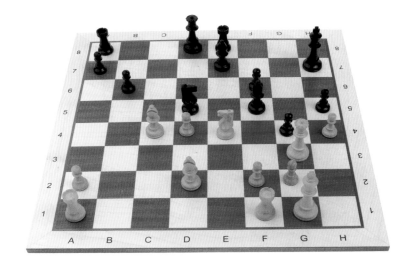

White's move is relatively easy this time, with Qg3-b3—the most logical move. On b3, the Queen augments the pressure along the a2-g8 diagonal. Black is simply unable to defend the Knight a second time. If, for example, black plays Bg6-f7, white can play Ne4-c3, a third attack on the poor Nd5. If the black Knight on d5 were to move, the black Bishop on f7 would fall.

Black therefore retreats the Nd5 to c7, three squares away from the c4-Bishop, in an effort to limit the Bishop's scope.

After 12 moves in this middlegame, white has a substantial advantage. You might imagine continuing with Ra1-c1 or Bc4-f7. Both are excellent moves. Ra1-c1 places white's final undeveloped piece on an open file. White's Bc4-f7 takes advantage of the entry square on f7. Note that after Bg6xf7, the white Queen would powerfully infiltrate the black Kingside on the f7 square. White's strategy has resulted in a nice range of options that gives white by far the best chances to win the game.

In the actual game (J. Edwards vs. W. Jones, 1993), the contest ended as follows:

```
28.Bc4-f7   Re8-f8
29.Bf7xg6+  Kh7xg6
30.Ne4-g3   Rf8-h8
31.Ra1-c1   Nc7-e8
32.Qb3-e6   Be7-a3
33.Ng3xh5   Ba3xc1
34.Qe6xg4+  Kg6-f7
35.Qg4-e6+  Kf7-g6
36.Nh5-f4+  Kg6-h7
37.Qe6-f7+  Ne8-g7
38.Nf4-h5   1–0
```

Black resigns.

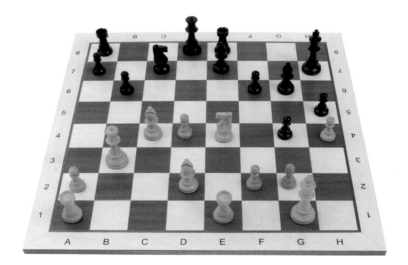

Responding to Threats

Strong moves often contain threats. A threat is simply the move that you would make if, after having moved, you were given an opportunity to make a second consecutive move. When your opponent makes a move that contains a threat, you have an important choice: Stop the threat immediately, or make a move that contains a bigger threat. In the following sequence, the moves on both sides contain numerous threats.

A Sequence of Threats

This scenario occurred in the Sicilian Defense after the moves 1.e2-e4 c7-c5, 2.Ng1-f3 Nb8-c6, 3.d2-d4 c5xd4, 4.Nf3xd4 Ng8-f6, 5.Nb1-c3 e7-e5. Black's last move, e7-e5, threatens on the next move to capture white's Nd4. White has many options for the Knight, including the retreat to f3, but white prefers to play Nd4-b5, where the Knight will threaten the move Nb5-d6 check. Black responds by stopping that threat with the move d7-d6.

You might recognize that black's central pawn structure contains a weakness on d6 and a central hole on d5. White would like to play the move Nc3-d5 but the Nd5 would be captured immediately by the strong Nf6. Rather than play the move Nd5, white threatens to play it by first moving Bc1-g5. The Bishop pins the Nf6 to the black Queen and the threat of Nc3-d5 is now real.

Strong players often say that "the threat is stronger than the execution." They mean that preparing the threat correctly (in this position with Bc1-g5) is better than playing the threat immediately (with Nc3-d5) as you can see in this position.

After the move Bc1-g5, black has several interesting candidate moves. Black could un-pin immediately with Bf8-e7. Black could guard the d5-square with Bc8-e6. But black prefers to meet the threat of Nc3-d5 with his own threat, the move a7-a6 threatening to capture the Nb5.

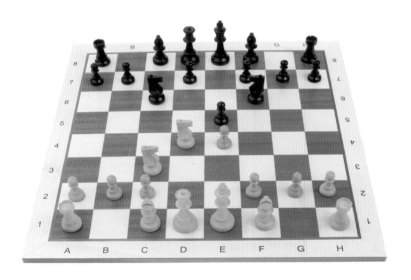

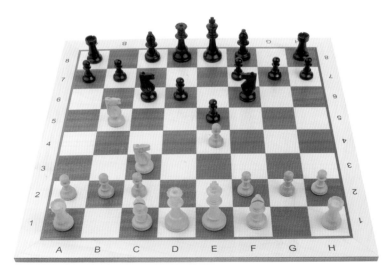

White's Nb5 is now under attack and has only one logical retreat. White could play Bg5xf6, meeting the threat on the Nb5 with a larger threat, but black might simply recapture with the g7-pawn. White therefore retreats the Nb5-a3. Black responds with b7-b5, a move that carries another threat, a pawn fork with b5-b4.

White stops the threat of the pawn fork on b4 simply by moving the Nc3 powerfully to the central hole on d5. The black Nf6 dare not capture the Nd5 because the Bg5 is pinning it to the black Queen. Black therefore responds with Bf8-e7, a move that carries another threat, this time the move Nf6xNd5, winning a piece!

CONTINUED ON NEXT PAGE

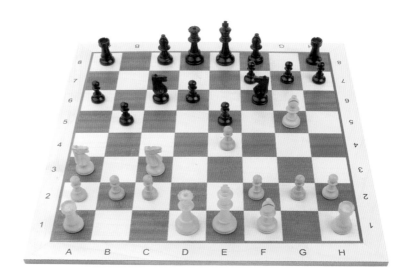

Responding to Threats *(continued)*

Responding to the threat, white now plays Bg5xf6, giving up the Bg5 but stopping the threat of Nf6xd5 and retaining the powerful Nd5. To advance in chess, watch carefully for such threats. Strong chess players develop a finely honed sense of danger. Before you move, always ask: "Does my opponent's last move contain a threat?" If so, your move should either stop the threat or, even better, you should look for a threat that's even bigger.

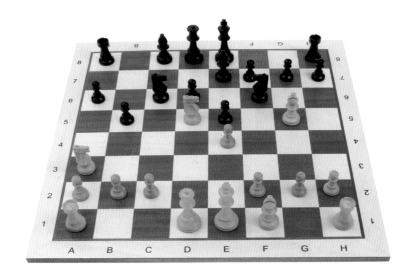

Meeting a Threat with a Bigger Threat

Sometimes, the best way to meet a threat is with an even bigger threat. In this position, white has just made the move Nc3-d5. The Nd5 threatens to capture the Qf6 and threatens to play Nd5xc7 check, forking the black King and the Ra8. You might expect black to meet both threats with the move Qf6-d8, removing the Queen from attack and using the Queen to defend the c7-pawn.

Instead, black responds to the threat of Nd5xc7 with a bigger threat: Qf6-g6.

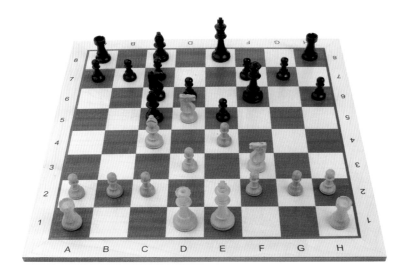

The move Qf6-g6 may surprise you, and you might wonder where black's threat is. Let's take a look. If white is insensitive to the danger, white might continue with Nd5xc7 check. In check, black would move the King to d8.

With the Nc7 under attack from the King, white would continue with Nc7xa8. But now, black would be able to demonstrate that the Qf6-g6 move had considerable bite. Black continues with Qg6xg2.

CONTINUED ON NEXT PAGE

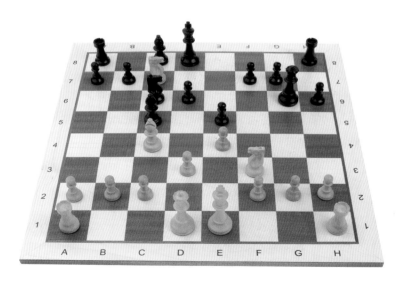

The power of black's idea is now clear. On g2, the Queen threatens both the white Rh1 as well as Qg2xf2 checkmate! To prevent both threats, white must move the Rh1-f1. Black would likely respond with the powerful move Bc8-g4, pinning and soon winning white's Nf3.

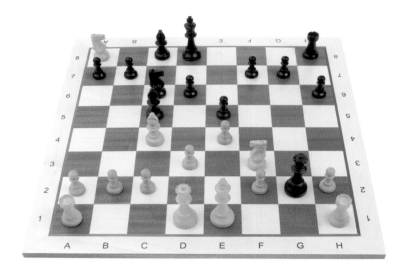

With the threats of Bg4xf3 and Nc6-d4 along with the idea of capturing the Na8 by moving the King and then playing Rh8xa8, black is well ahead.

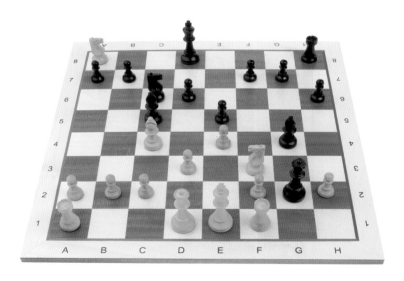

Almost every time that someone captures one of your pieces, you will want to recapture. There are exceptions, however, and there is nothing automatic about recapturing. Always consider other options.

Recapturing Your Pieces and Pawns

In this position, black's advantage is pronounced. The Nd5 is in the center the board where it can't be attacked by white's pawns. White's dark-squared Bishop on d2 is bad, locked in by its own pawns. By contrast, the black Bishop on d8 will have an important role to play in black's attack on the Kingside. Note that black's Rooks are actively doubled on the g-file and the Qh6 is bearing down on the white Kingside.

In an effort to relieve some of the pressure in this position, white played Bc4xd5. Most chess players would gladly recapture immediately with the e6-pawn in order to undouble the black e-pawns. But black has a much stronger response with the move Rg5-h5.

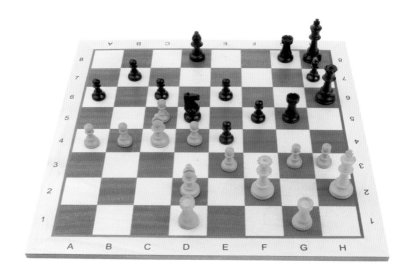

Black suddenly has the huge threat of a check with Rh5xh3+, forcing the white King to g2. Then white can play Rh5-h2, checking the Kg2 and then winning the white Qf2 with check when the King retreats to f1. Masters achieve their strength in part because they consistently look for such "in-between" moves.

chapter 12

Elementary Checkmates

To win a chess game, you must deliver a checkmate (or mate, for short)—placing your opponent's King in check with the King having no legal move. In this chapter, you will be able to explore all the most basic checkmates. As you will see, some of these checkmates are very simple. In fact, if you're clever enough to Queen a pawn, the checkmate with two Queens against a lone King is easy and fun to do. The other checkmates in this chapter are somewhat more challenging, but with a bit of practice, you'll be able to deliver checkmate with just a Rook or even with a King, Bishop, and Knight.

You will also learn to recognize when there is insufficient material to deliver a checkmate. That way, you won't play on and on, trying to do the impossible. Or perhaps when you're trailing, you will be able to reach such an endgame and avoid a loss.

Two Queens

You can have more than one Queen by promoting pawns. Some players enjoy promoting more than two, if they can, but two Queens are almost always enough to deliver checkmate. In this section, you will see how two Queens together are so powerful that checkmates will occur quite quickly.

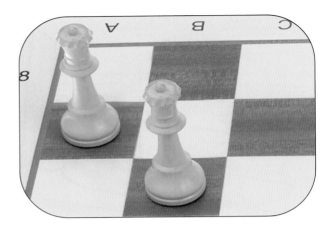

The Basic Checkmate

Here is the basic checkmate. With white to move, white can deliver a check on several squares, but the move Qb6-b8 is checkmate. On b8, the Queen will be attacking the black King, which cannot escape from the attack. Note that the Queen on a7 controls all of the squares of the 7th rank while, after Qb6-b8, the Queen on b8 controls all of the squares of the 8th rank.

How to Get There

The simplest method for this checkmate is illustrated here. The technique is a bit like walking a dog, forcing the King step by step toward the top edge of the board. Here, white has many paths to the checkmate, but the simplest is clearly Qb4-b6, attacking the lone King. The King must retreat to the 7th rank.

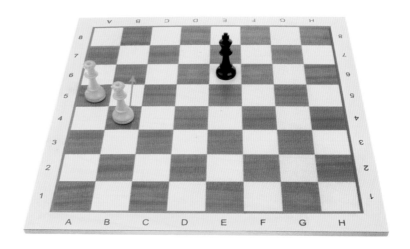

Here, after the retreat of the King to d7, white will continue to force the King toward the top of the board by playing Qa5-a7. Note that, given the power of the white Queens, the black King is unable to approach the Queens in an effort to prevent the checkmate.

After Qa5-a7, you will be in the same position illustrated at the beginning of this section (see the previous page). As you can see, checkmating with two Queens is relatively simple.

CONTINUED ON NEXT PAGE

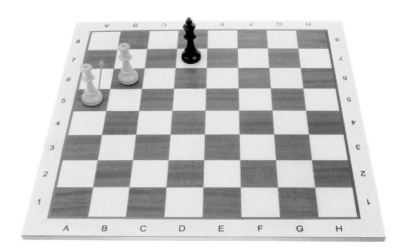

Another Way to Checkmate

Here is another example of a checkmate with two Queens. White could simply proceed with the technique we just reviewed, but there is a much faster and more elegant checkmate. The Qb5 controls the 5th rank while the Qc3 controls the 3rd rank.

White begins with Qb5-e5 check. Note that, after the check, black has only a single legal move, to g4.

White completes the checkmate by playing Qc3-g3#, using the Queen on e5 to support the Qg3. It is a beautiful checkmate!

In many chess games, however, you might not have the luxury of having so much extra material. In the following sections, we will explore checkmates with less material.

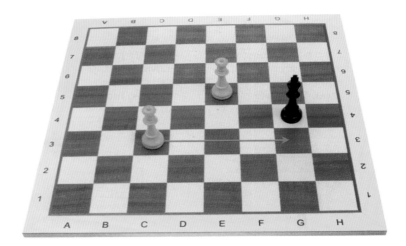

Together, the Queen and Rook are almost as powerful as the two Queens. And in most chess games, you are more likely to have a Queen and Rook in an endgame than two Queens. Both techniques that you saw in the first section are still useful here.

How to Get There

THE FIRST TECHNIQUE

In this position, the Queen and Rook combine very much like the two Queens. White brings about a quick checkmate by playing Qa5-a7 and then, once the King retreats to the 8th rank, with Rb6-b8 checkmate.

Black has no choice but to retreat along the 4th rank to f4. White continues with Qc5-e5 check, driving the King farther along the 4th rank to g4. The technique should be clear now. White alternates Rook and Queen moves, driving the King to the edge of the board.

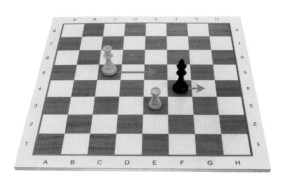

THE SECOND TECHNIQUE

This position requires a slightly different technique. Here, the Queen covers all the squares on the 5th rank, while the Rook covers the 3rd rank. White begins by playing Rc3-e3 check. Note that the Qc5 defends the Rook on e3.

Checkmate is near. White continues, with the Re3-g3 check, driving the King to the edge on h4. White then follows with the Qe5-g5 checkmate. The Queen and Rook are defending each other while covering all of the King's possible retreats.

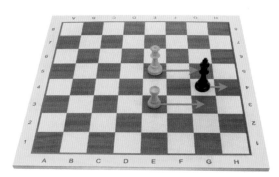

Two Rooks

Using two Rooks is another common checkmate. It is slightly more difficult to do because the Rooks are not as powerful as the Queens.

How to Get There

The Rooks will attempt to walk the black King toward the 8th rank. This time, however, the King will be able to approach the Rooks and disrupt the simple checkmate. White begins as expected by playing Ra4-a6, forcing the black King to retreat toward the 8th rank.

As you can see, the King retreated to the d7-square, approaching the Rooks. As with the Queens, white continues with Rb5-b7, forcing the black King to the top edge of the board.

Black moved Kd7-c8, attacking Rb7. The Rooks do not support each other like the two Queens and the Queen and Rook did. If white carelessly played Ra6-a8 check, black could escape with Kc8xRb7. Instead, white safeguards the Rb7 by moving it across the 7th rank to h7.

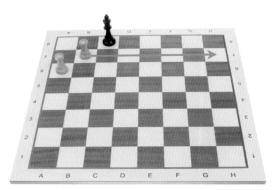

With the threat of Ra6-a8 checkmate looming, black must defend the a8-square by playing Kc8-b8. The defense is annoying, but white can still win by shifting the a6-Rook toward the Kingside with Ra6-g6. Facing the inevitable move Rg6-g8 checkmate, black might resign here. Few chess players like being checkmated.

King and Queen

It might surprise you to learn that the Queen alone cannot deliver checkmate. When it's down to King and Queen vs. the King, the Queen requires close cooperation with its King to deliver the mate.

A Simple Checkmate

Here is the simplest of the checkmates with a Queen and a King. Notice that the Qd7 is smothering the black King against the top edge of the board. Simply put, the Queen is attacking the King and covering all the black King's possible retreats. Moreover, the black King cannot capture the Queen because the Qd7 is defended by the white King.

CONTINUED ON NEXT PAGE

Other Ways to Checkmate

In this position, white can bring about a similar checkmate by playing Qg7-e7 checkmate. Even though the white King is on d6, the Queen on e7 will still be defended and will be smothering the black King against the edge of the board. White has an additional option, playing Qg7-g8 checkmate. In this position, the white King is preventing a black retreat to d7 and e7, while the Queen not only attacks the black King but also covers the key d8, f8, and f7 squares.

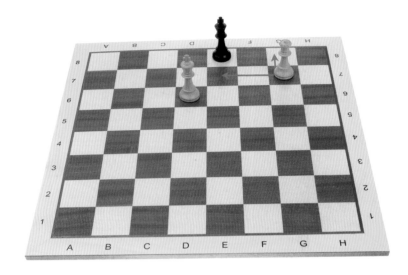

In this position, white again has two possible checkmates in one move. White can play either Qg2-a8 or Qg2-g8. Both moves attack the black King, and cover all of the squares on the 8th rank, while the white King prevents any move by the black King to the 7th rank.

Moves to Avoid

In bringing about the checkmate with your King and Queen, there are two key moves to avoid. In this position, white has a simple checkmate with Qb6-b8. However, Qb6-d6 is a move that many players make without realizing the danger.

With the white Queen on d6, black has been stalemated! Black of course must move, but black has no legal move and the black King is not in check. Note that stalemate applies only when one side has no legal move whatsoever. For more on stalemates, see the section "Stalemates and Other Draws" in Chapter 2. There are many positions in which the King or another piece cannot move. It is only a stalemate if one side is not in check and has no legal moves anywhere on the board.

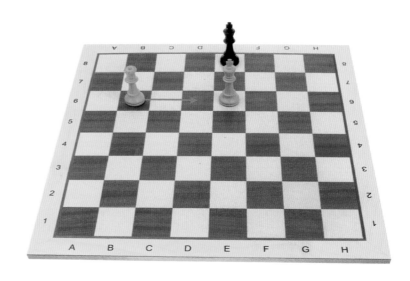

In this interesting position, white should march the white King toward f6 and deliver checkmate with the Queen. This strategy speaks to the key of all of these King and Queen checkmates: To win, the King and Queen must work together in harmony. Instead, white blundered with Qa7-f7?, again with a stalemate.

Notice that the black King is not in check. But because of the bad move by the white Queen, the black King has no legal moves.

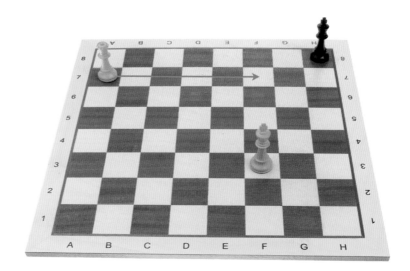

Mating with a Rook is somewhat more challenging than mating with a Queen, although many players prefer this mate because there are fewer possibilities for a stalemate.

The Basic Checkmate

Here is the basic checkmate. The Rf8 is checking the black King and preventing Kh8-g8. As in the King and Queen endgames, the white King plays an essential role by preventing the black King from escaping to either g7 or h7.

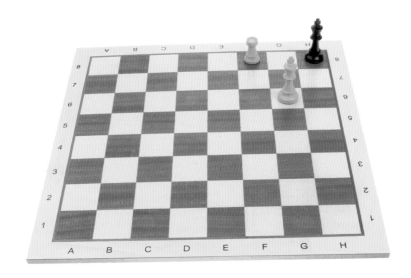

Backing up just one move, the checkmate in this position should be clear. White simply advances the Rook from f7 to f8 checkmate. A significant mistake would be Rf7-g7, resulting in the only stalemate with a King and Rook. Therefore, it is a key move to avoid.

Here, if it were black's move, the black King would have only one move—Kg8-h8. White would then checkmate with Rf7-f8 as we have seen.

But if it is white's move, white wants to make sure that the black King does not escape to the Queenside. White therefore plays Rf7-f1. Actually, any backward movement of the Rook along the f-file would accomplish the purpose, but most chess players like dramatic finishes.

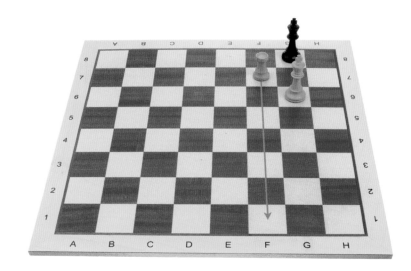

Black has no choice in this position but to move the King directly into the corner at h8. With a flourish, white can play Rf1-f8, delivering checkmate.

CONTINUED ON NEXT PAGE

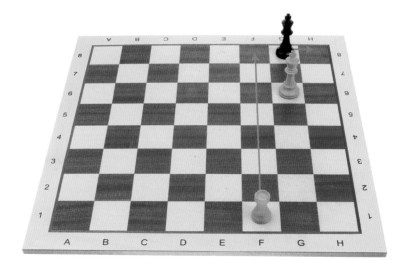

How to Get There

Checkmating with a King and Rook is easy once the King is in the corner. Here's how you can force the enemy King into the corner. Notice that the white Re5 has already placed the black King in a box. The Rook controls e6, e7, and e8, as well as the key squares on the 5th rank: f5, g5, and h5. The black King is trapped inside those squares and has only nine squares at its disposal (f6, f7, f8, g6, g7, g8, h6, h7, and h8).

To make some headway, the white King and Rook must work together. White begins with Ke4-f4, waiting for the black King to move backward.

Black is in a quandary. If black moves to g6, white has Re5-f5 to push black further toward the corner and close the box from nine squares to just six (g6, g7, g8, h6, h7, and h8). Therefore, black decides to move instead to f7.

The moment that black gives ground, white should step forward to claim that territory. In this case, white has the strong move Kf4-f5, claiming control over both f6 and g6.

Fearing an imminent checkmate, black does not want to retreat to the top edge of the board. Rather, black tries to hold ground with Kf7-g7.

White could continue slowly with Re5-e6 and, indeed, you might want to practice such a slow procedure. As it turns out, white can proceed more quickly here with a check Re5-e7 check. Black might not want to respond by moving the King to f8 where, after Kf5-f6, white is very close to the checkmate that introduced this section. Instead, black tries to escape from the corner with Kg7-h6.

In this position, white moves toward the end of the game quickly with a dramatic Re7-a7 (other Rook moves to b7, c7, d7, or f7 also work), forcing the black King to move to h5.

At the end of a long sequence, white has a beautiful checkmate in one move with Ra7-h7. As you can see, these checkmates require patience. Of course, it helps to recognize the mating patterns. You will find that, after a bit of practice, you will be able to deliver checkmate with just a King and a Rook.

King and Two Bishops

A checkmate with two Bishops does not occur often. If it does, you will find that patience is required. The first step is to force the King toward any edge of the board and then toward any corner. The checkmate will look very much like the photo on the right. Notice that the white King is playing a very active role in blocking the escape of the black King. The light-squared Bishop is controlling the g8 escape square. The dark-squared Bishop is attacking the black King and delivering the checkmate.

How to Get There

1.Be4-f5 Ke7-d8

There are many ways to proceed in this position. White would like to drive the black King toward the top edge of the board and then walk the King into one of the corners. Black would like to try to run away from white's King and Bishop and therefore might try Ke7-d7. White therefore begins with 1.Be4-f5 to prevent black from moving to d7. Black continues to try to escape toward the a-file with Ke7-d8.

Note: *As you learned in the "Chess Notation" section in Chapter 1, the move number is indicated with a numeral followed by a period at the beginning of the notation. Here, we use move numbers starting with "1." to best illustrate this endgame scenario. These move numbers are not indicative of a start-to-finish game, but are instead used to easily illustrate the order of moves necessary to achieve this checkmate.*

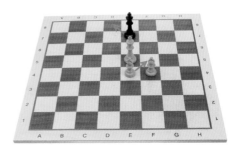

2.Ke5-d6 Kd8-e8

White prevents any further movement of the black King toward the Queenside by advancing the King from e5 to d6. Black has no choice but to continue with Kd8-e8.

3.Bf4-g5 Ke8-f7

Here, white's move Bf4-g5 captures control over the d8-square and prevents the black King from moving toward the Queenside. Black responds by moving off the 8th rank with Ke8-f7 to try to hold on to as much territory as possible.

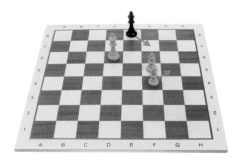

4.Kd6-d7 Kf7-f8

In turn, white takes control over the e8-square that black vacated by advancing Kd6-d7. Black again tries to avoid moving toward the corner with Kf7-f8.

5.Kd7-e6 Kf8-e8

White progresses with the King toward the key g6-square. Black again tries to escape toward the Queenside, Kf8-e8.

CONTINUED ON NEXT PAGE

6.Bf5-g6+ Ke8-f8

White regains control over the e8-square, forcing the black King toward the corner with Bf5-g6+. To get out of check, black's King makes its only legal move, Ke8-f8.

7.Bg5-h6 Kf8-g8

White's dark-squared Bishop moves aggressively to h6 to control both the f8 and g7 squares. Black again makes the only legal move it has, Kf8-g8.

8.Bg6-e4 Kg8-h8

White moves the light-squared Bishop to e4 where it continues to control the h7 escape square but also readies the idea of Be4-d5. Black is forced to move the King to h8.

9.Ke6-f6 Kh8-g8

White brings its King closer to the g6-square where it can control the g7 and h7 squares without help from the Bishops. Black again moves back to g8.

10.Kf6-g6 Kg8-h8

The movement back and forth is not a threefold repetition because white's moves have been different. Indeed, white continues to make progress, with the King having reached the key g6-square. Black retreats again to h8.

11.Bh6-g7+ Kh8-g8

White moves Bh6-g7 for check and is very close to checkmate. White's Bg7+ move forces the black King back to g8 where, suddenly, it has no moves.

12.Be4-d5 checkmate

White's Be4-d5 is a pretty checkmate.

King, Bishop, and Knight

Of all the checkmates in this chapter, the checkmate with a King, Bishop, and Knight is the most complex. It is so difficult that some masters have failed to deliver the checkmate within the 50-move limit rule. (The U.S. Chess Federation rule book states that the result of a game is a draw if, after 50 consecutive moves by each player, there have been no captures or pawn moves.)

The Final Checkmate Position

Here is the final checkmate. Note that the white King controls the g7 and h7 escape squares. The Nh6 plays a key role in controlling g8. And of course, the Bd4 is delivering the final check. The key to this endgame is that the checkmate can be forced only in the corner that the Bishop can control. Players with the lone King should therefore run into the "wrong" corner and see if their opponent can figure out how to force the checkmate.

How to Get There

In this position, white has already made good progress. The black King is on the edge of the board. White needs to decide which corner to drive the black King into.

1.Be5-f6 Ke8-f8

Be5-f6 prevents the black King from moving to d8 and toward the wrong corner. Black's response to f8 is black's only legal move.

2.Bf6-e7+ Kf8-g8

The Bishop check on e7 forces the black King to g8 because Kf8-e8 would allow Nf5-d6 checkmate!

3.Ke6-f6 Kg8-h7

The white King heads toward the key g6-square, moving Ke6-f6. Black moves the King to Kg8-h7 to prevent white from moving to g6 and in an effort to run the King toward h1.

CONTINUED ON NEXT PAGE

4.Kf6-f7 Kh7-h8

White makes a "waiting move" with Kf6-f7, knowing that black will have no choice but to leave the h7-square, moving Kh7-h8.

5.Kf7-g6 Kh8-g8

The white King has reached the g6-square with Kf7-g6. The black King has no choice but to shuttle back and forth between g8 and h8.

6.Nf5-h6+ Kg8-h8

The white Knight moves to h6, delivering check and forcing the black King into the correct corner. The final move of the game will be 7.Be7-f6 checkmate, a beautiful final position.

Insufficient Mating Material

Please note that it is not possible to force a checkmate with just a Bishop or just a Knight. Even with a King and two Knights, no checkmate can be forced. In this position, white will be able to deliver checkmate if black plays the Kg8 into the h8-corner. But black can avoid all trouble simply by playing Kg8-f8.

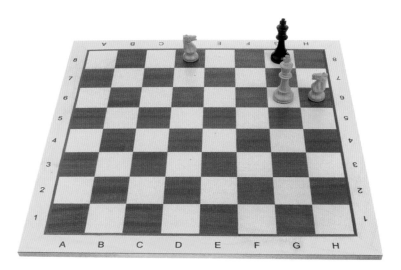

TIP

Use a Chess Database to Help Your Game

A chess database is simply a database that is dedicated to chess. These specialized chess applications provide you with easy access to the history of chess. Current programs come with more than 3,000,000 games that you can view and play through.

For example, you can use ChessBase, the most popular of these programs (www.chessbase.com) to find all the games of your favorite players and the games in your favorite openings. You can even play through an assortment of great combinations or instructive endgames. The PlayChess website (www.playchess.com) has a unique feature: All the games that you play there will be entered in the ChessBase database. This enables you to explore what other players did in the same position, or simply what you did wrong in a key position.

In ChessBase, you can view a board position that shows the different moves that have been played from this position, as well as statistical information with regard to the relative success of the different alternatives. There is also an interesting list of the grandmasters who have favored each alternative and a list of all the games actually played from this position. With a chess database, you can easily play through many important games very quickly, learning as you go.

Attacking the King

The most exciting phase of the game of chess is the attacks leading to checkmate or to the gain of substantial material. In this chapter, you will be able to review a number of different patterns for attacking an opponent. By playing through these patterns, you will learn to recognize such possibilities in your own game—either how to bring about the attacks or how to stop them.

In almost every section, you will see that the black King, as checkmate approaches, has no moves. As a general rule, when your opponent's King cannot move, all you need is check! Many strong players use this rule. When they reach positions in which their opponent's King cannot move, they know that they can safely sacrifice considerable material if they can find a way to deliver the final blow.

Note: As I did in the later sections of Chapter 12, "Elementary Checkmates," I again show these checkmates move by move, starting the move numbering with "1." Again, these move numbers are not indicative of a start-to-finish game, but are instead used to easily illustrate the order of the moves necessary to achieve these checkmates.

Smothered Mate

The smothered checkmate is one of the prettiest in chess. A lone Knight, with help from the enemy forces, checkmates the King. As you can see here, with the smothered mate, the black King is under attack and cannot move because its own Rook and pawns are blocking the escape.

The Smothered Mate in Action

1.Ng5-f7+ Kh8-g8

Are you wondering why the black player would have allowed such a powerful move? The actual checkmate usually begins in a position like this one. As you can see, the black Rook is not on g8 and would certainly not want to move there voluntarily.

White begins by moving the Ng5-f7, giving check to the black King. The King has no choice but to move out of the corner to g8.

2.Nf7-h6++ Kg8-h8

The power of the double check! White continues by moving the Nf7-h6, giving check to the black King from both Nh6 and Qb3. Black cannot capture the white Knight with the g7-pawn because the black King is also in check from the Queen.

Black must move its King, but not to f8 where the white Queen, supported by the Nh6, would deliver checkmate with 3.Qb3-f7. The black King therefore retreats back into the corner.

Note: As you learned in Chapter 1 in the section on "Chess Notation," A single "+" after a move indicates a check. In turn, "++" indicates a double check.

3.Qb3-g8+ Ra8xg8

Rather than check again with the Knight on f7, white plays the amazing Qb3-g8+. Black cannot capture the Queen with the its King because the Knight on h6 supports the g8 square. Black therefore must capture on g8 with the Rook.

4.Nh6-f7 Checkmate

White's final move of Nh6-f7# is pleasing to the eye. Watch for such combinations in your own games. You might be surprised how often this smothered checkmate occurs in practice.

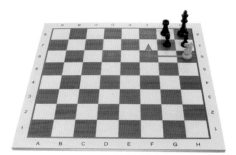

FAQ

I'd like to play in a chess tournament, but how do I find one?

Every year, thousands of chess tournaments are held, including dozens in every state. Tournaments are the best place to meet other players and to practice the craft of chess. Most tournament events are certified by the United States Chess Federation (www.uschess.org), and the games are rated. The better your results, the higher your rating. With a high enough rating, you can gain an official title of expert, master, or even grandmaster.

The U.S. Chess Federation publishes a monthly magazine, *Chess Life,* and maintains a website, both of which list tournaments throughout the United States. Their Web page www.uschess.org/directories/tnmtsearch/ permits you to search for tournaments in your area. State and regional championships tend to be the most competitive events, but there are club and weekend events that attract a wide range of players.

Back Rank Mate

The back rank mate is both simple and elegant. The white Rook checks the King along the back rank, and black's own pawns prevent the King from escaping, as shown here. In practice, the back rank mate can be easy or surprisingly difficult. There are two examples in this section: the first easy, the second more difficult.

The Back Rank Mate in Action

AN EASY BACK RANK MATE

1.Qe3-e7+ Kf8-g8

In this position, white does not have a direct checkmate if it moves its Queen to the e8-square because the black King on f8 and the Rook on d8 both help to defend e8. White therefore first plays the Queen to the e7-square in order to drive the black King back to g8.

2.Qe7-e8+ Rd8xe8

The rest is simple. White has two attacks on the key e8-square. Black has only the Rook defending. White therefore sacrifices the Queen on e8 with Qe7-e8+, forcing Black to capture with Rd8xe8.

3.Re1xe8 Checkmate

Although white has lost the Queen, the result is clear. The white Rook moves to e8 to capture black's Rook. This move is checkmate, because the black King, thanks to its own pawns, has no escape.

A MORE DIFFICULT BACK RANK MATE

1.Qf2xf7+ Rf8xf7

Here is a somewhat more challenging example of the back rank checkmate. Notice first that white has three attacks on the black f7-pawn, while black has only two defenses. White could therefore begin with 1.Ra7xf7, although there would be no immediate checkmate if black responded with Rg6-f6.

White begins instead with the neat Queen sacrifice on f7 (Qf2xf7+). In check, black cannot simply retreat the King into the corner or white will checkmate quickly with 2.Qf7xf8 checkmate. Black therefore must capture the Queen with Rf8xf7.

2.Ra7-a8+ Rf7-f8

At first glance, it might appear that white has simply lost a Queen. But don't forget about the back rank checkmate. White plays Ra7-a8, delivering check to the Kg8. Black could bring the Queen back to d8, but white would simply capture the Queen. Black therefore blocks the check by retreating Rf7-f8.

3. Ra8xf8 or Rf1xf8 Checkmate

To end the game, white will capture the black Rf8 with either of its Rooks (Ra8xf8 or Rf1xf8)—checkmate!

Gueridon Mate

Here is another very pleasing check-mate in which the King's own forces block its escape. The white Queen is attacking the King. The King cannot capture the Queen because the pawn on e5 defends it. The two black Rooks are occupying the only escape squares that the Queen doesn't directly control.

The Gueridon Mate in Action

1.Bc4xf7+ Ke8xf7

Some combinations seem to come from nowhere. White does have excellent control over the center and appears to be ready to castle and to play Nb1-c3.

Instead, white launches a power attack on the black King with Bc4xf7+. The f7-pawn, defended only by the black King, is black's weakest pawn. Black could decline the sacrifice and opt not to recapture with the King, but that would leave black's King on f8 and white would be able to fork the black King and Queen with Nd4-e6+. So black recaptures the Bishop with Ke8xf7.

2.Nd4-e6 Kf7xe6

White presses forward with the amazing Nd4-e6, threatening the black Queen. Note that black could simply move the Qd8 to safety on e8. Doing so, however, would invite Ne6xc7, forking the Rook and Queen, and white would probably continue to attack with Qd1-d5. Instead, black, noticing that the advanced white Knight is undefended on e6, captures it with the King.

3.Qd1-d5+ Ke6-f6

It is extremely dangerous to move a King so early into the middle of the board. White is quick to punish the black King. White continues with Qd1-d5 check, attacking the black King with support from its e4-pawn. Black, blocked by a pawn, a Knight, and a Bishop, has only one legal move: Ke6-f6.

4.Qd5-f5 Checkmate

The white Queen delivers the Gueridon checkmate with Qd5-f5. The white Queen smothers the black King, with black's own pieces blocking the escape.

FACT

From the French word for pedestal, the Gueridon mate is likely of French origin. If you prefer, this checkmate is sometimes referred to as the Swallow's Tail mate.

Greco's Mate

Greco's mate is very much like the back rank mate, but on the side of the board instead. As you can see here, the white Rook is attacking the King along the h-file. The white Bishop on b3 controls the g8 escape square, while the black pawn on g7 prevents the King from moving there. Checkmate.

Greco's Mate in Action

1.Ne5-g6+ h7xg6

At first glance, it might appear that white is in trouble. After all, the black Knight on d2 is forking the white Qf3 and the Rf1. However, notice that the white Bb3 is cutting straight through to the g8-square, preventing the black King from moving.

White begins by checking with the e5-Knight to g6. This Knight check would be checkmate, except that black can capture the Knight with its h7-pawn. Black has no choice but to accept this Knight sacrifice (h7xg6).

2.Qf3-h3 Checkmate

White ends the game quickly with Qh3 checkmate, a pretty example of Greco's mate.

Epaulette Mate

A Rook or a Queen provides the final check in this pleasing checkmate. In this position, the Rook delivers a check along the open g-file. The poor black King has no escape; it's hemmed in by the two black Rooks and the f- and h-pawns.

Epaulette Mate in Action

The Epaulette mate is a useful part of your chess arsenal. Positions like this can occur if the enemy King, rather than castling, is forced by a check to walk toward its own Rook.

1.Qe7xf6 g7xf6

Black's position looks secure, but white will win quickly, starting with Qe7xf6. The Queen capture pries open the black Kingside. Black is not forced to recapture and, indeed other moves would permit the game to go on. Nonetheless, the winning of a Knight is very useful and usually enough to guarantee victory. Black therefore responds with g7xf6.

2.Rd3-g3 Checkmate

Now that the g7-pawn has captured the white Queen on f6, the g-file is open for the white Rook to deliver the checkmate. Once white plays Rd3-g3, the King is in check. Black cannot capture or block the Rook, and the black King has no escape from the check. It's checkmate!

Anastasia's Mate

Anastasia's checkmate is very similar to a back rank mate except that it can occur on any side of the board. As you can see in the final position of Anastasia's mate shown here, the Rook along the h-file is delivering checkmate. The white Knight has control over the g6 and g8 escape squares, while the black pawn on g7 blocks the King's other escape square.

Anastasia's Mate in Action

Try to imagine how to achieve Anastasia's checkmate from this position. Clearly, white will need to check with the Knight on e7 and pry open the h-file for the checkmate.

1.Nf5-e7+ Kg8-h8

With white to move, it plays the Knight to e7 check, which forces the black King into the corner at h8. After black's move, note that the black King cannot move. All white needs is to check.

2.Rh1xh7+ Kh8xh7

White blasts through the black defense with a nice Rook sacrifice on h7. Black has no choice but to recapture the Rook with its King. The mate is now set up. The white Knight on e7 controls both g8 and g6, while the black pawn blocks any escape by the black King to g7.

3.Qd2-h2 Checkmate

White ends the game with Anastasia's mate, this time with the check from the Queen on h2.

Boden's Mate

In 1853, an Englishman named Samuel Boden was the first to uncork this fascinating finish. The black King has castled Queenside and has no moves because the white Bh2 cuts through the dark-square diagonal all the way to b8.

Boden's Mate at a Glance

1.Qf3xc6+ b7xc6

White begins with Qf3xc6+, a spectacular Queen sacrifice that rips open the black Queenside. The black King cannot move to b8 because the Bh2 controls the b8-h2 diagonal, and there is no way to block the check. Black therefore has no choice but to accept the sacrifice by capturing the Queen, b7xc6.

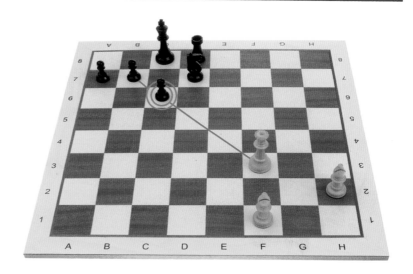

2.Bf1-a6 Checkmate

The game ends abruptly with the check from the light-squared Bishop, Bf1-a6. Notice how the two Bishops by themselves deliver this pleasing checkmate.

CONTINUED ON NEXT PAGE

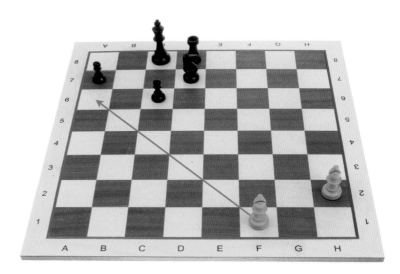

Boden's Mate in Action

This position seems ripe for Boden's mate. Note that black has castled on the Queenside and that the black King cannot move. However, the white Knight on b5 is blocking the Bd3's access to the a6-square. How can white deliver the mate?

1.Nb5xa7+ Bb8xa7

White begins by ditching the Nb5, capturing the pawn on a7 and forcing black to recapture with the Bb8. Once the exchange on a7 occurs, you will start to recognize Boden's mate.

2.Qf3xc6+ b7xc6

In this example, there is no Queen sacrifice, simply an exchange of Queens on the c6-square. But the result is the same. White's light-squared Bishop now has access to the key a6-square.

3.Bd3-a6 Checkmate

The a6-square is now open for the checkmate. Even though there wasn't a true Queen sacrifice here (black and white just exchanged Queens), the final checkmate is still very satisfying.

Blackburne's Mate

Joseph Henry Blackburne, a 19th-century English master who was nicknamed the Black Death, discovered this nice checkmate with two Bishops. Note here that the two Bishops are actively cutting through the position toward the black King. The Knight on g5 plays a key role in the checkmate by supporting Bd3-h7 checkmate.

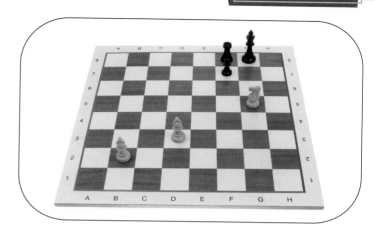

Blackburne's Mate in Action

Blackburn's mate often occurs when the g- and h-pawns advance in front of the King. As you can see here, white's Bb2 has control over all of the dark squares along the long diagonal. White would like to play Bd3-h7 checkmate but the pawn on g6 is in the way.

1.Qd1xh5 g6xh5

White begins with a Queen sacrifice that black simply cannot refuse. The Qd1xh5 threatens both Qh5-h7 checkmate and the Qh5-h8 checkmate. Once the g6xh5 recapture has occurred, the Bishop's diagonals are fully open.

2.Bd3-h7 Checkmate

In this example, white offered a Queen sacrifice to open lines for a Blackburn's checkmate. Bishop d3-h7 finishes the job. The fault here, of course, is black's for having weakened its Kingside with the advance of both the g- and h-pawns.

Lolli's Mate

Named after an 18th-century Italian chess enthusiast, Lolli's mate is a familiar theme to beginning chess players. The checkmate will occur with the white Queen on g7, supported by a pawn on f6 or h6 or perhaps by a Bishop along the a1-h8 diagonal.

Lolli's Mate at a Glance

1.f5-f6 g7-g6

As you can see in this example, the advance of the white pawn to f6 will often serve to weaken the black pawn structure, whether or not the f-pawn is taken. Here, of course, with the Queen pinning the g7-pawn, the g7xf6 capture is illegal. White's f5-f6 pawn advance threatens checkmate on g7 with Qg5xg7. Because black is unable to use a piece to capture on f6 or to defend the g7-pawn, black will have to respond with g7-g6, further weakening the Kingside. As you know, every pawn move creates a weakness. In this case, the g7-g6 pawn push creates a significant weakness on the h6-square.

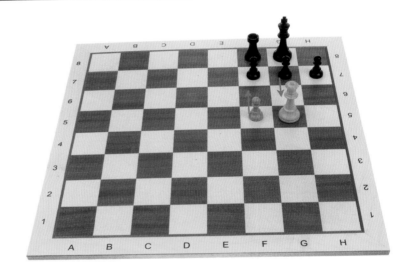

2.Qg5-h6 Kg8-h8

White takes immediate advantage of the new weakness on h6 to move the Queen there. The threat, often unstoppable, is the Qh6-g7 checkmate.

3.Qh6-g7 Checkmate

An abrupt finish. It's mate.

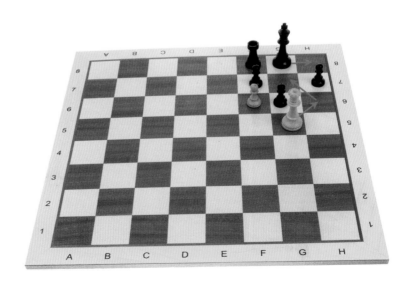

Lolli's Mate in Action

FIRST EXAMPLE

The threat of Lolli's mate often forces players to move the King into the corner and then to defend the g7 mating square with a Rook. Once again, this defense has left the black King without a move.

1.Qh6xh7 Kh8xh7

White, again, sacrifices the Queen with Qh6xh7 to expose the black King to further attack. It is generally not a good idea to give up your Queen unless you see clear compensation; with black recapturing with Kh8xh7 here, it's worth it.

2.Rf3-h3 Checkmate

In this case, the compensation is clear. The f6-pawn controls the g7 escape square, while the black Rg8 and the pawn on g6 also block the King's escape. Rf3-h3 is checkmate!

CONTINUED ON NEXT PAGE

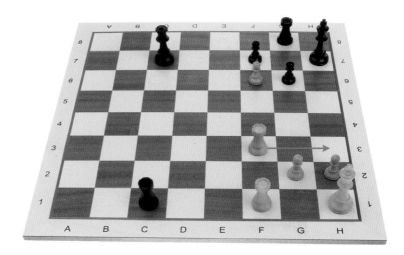

SECOND EXAMPLE

One additional feature of Lolli's mate is that, if the enemy Rook moves to g8 to prevent Qh6-g7 checkmate, the f7-pawn becomes weak. If a Knight were able to take safely on f7, the King, unable to move, would be checkmated.

1.Nf3-g5 Qf8xh6

Here, black appears to have defended successfully. The Rg8 prevents Qh6-g7 mate and the Qf8 defends the weak f7-pawn and challenges the white Queen on h6. White makes a very strong move, Nf3-g5, with the powerful threat Qh6xh7 checkmate. Black responds with Queen takes Queen in order to prevent the mate.

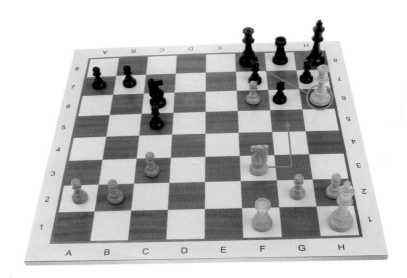

2.Ng5xf7 Checkmate

White unleashed a huge surprise—a smothered checkmate with the Knight!

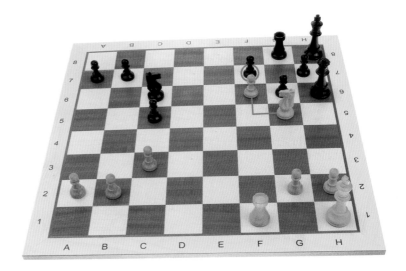

This common checkmate honors Harry Nelson Pillsbury, a great American player of the late 19th century. This mate takes advantage of a strong Bishop on the long diagonal and a Rook on an open g-file. In this simple position, white will capture on g7, but will it be with the Bishop or the Rook? Both appear strong, but one leads to checkmate in just two more moves.

Pillsbury's Mate at a Glance

1.Rg1xg7+ Kg8-h8

Here, white captures on g7 with the Rook because the black King is forced into the corner and white will now have a powerful discovered check.

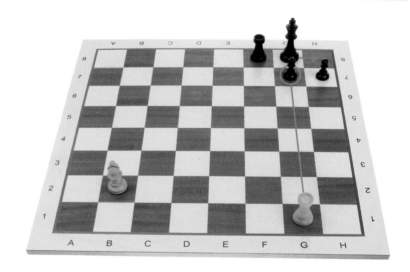

2.Rg7-g1+ Rf8-f6

White responds with Rg7-g1 for check (actually white could deliver check by withdrawing the Rook to any of the other squares along the g-file). The discovered check looks like mate but black can delay the inevitable by blocking the check with the Rf8-f6.

CONTINUED ON NEXT PAGE

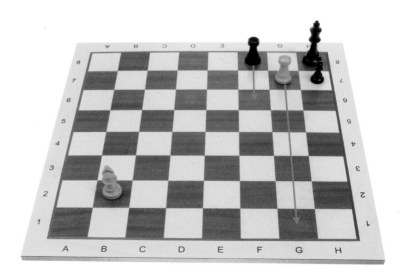

Pillsbury's Mate
(continued)

3.Bb2xf6 Checkmate

Another checkmate that is pleasing to the eye. The black King is jailed in the corner by the white Rook and the black pawn. The little Bishop delivers the final blow.

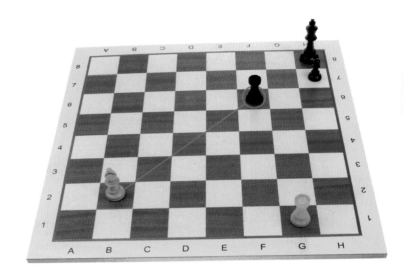

Pillsbury's Mate in Action

Despite black's material advantage, it is not surprising that white is winning in this position. The white Bishop on b2 has impressive control over the long diagonal, and the Rg1 has control over the open file pointed right at g7. Together, the Rook and Bishop are attacking the g7-pawn twice, and only the black King defends it. Note, however, that the black Knight on d3 is attacking the Bb2.

1.Rg1xg7+ Kg8-h8

White captures the g7-pawn in the most forceful way, with its Rook. Black has no choice but to move the King into the corner, permitting a discovered check on the next move. At least black can count on the fact that the Nd3 is attacking white's Bb2. On any conventional discovered check, black can simply play Nd3xb2.

2.Rg7-g8++ Kh8xg8

Rather than a discovered check, white tries a double check from both the Bb2 and the Rg8. The black King must move and, in fact, has only one move, to capture the Rg8.

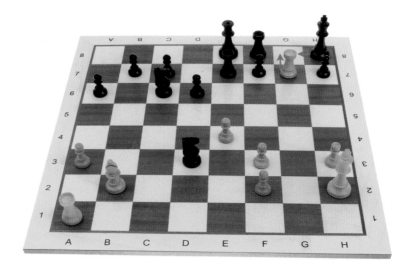

3.Ra1-g1 Checkmate

Here's Pillsbury's mate, a real beauty. Black cannot capture or block the check from the Rook. And of course, the black King on g8 cannot move, so the check from the Ra1-g1 is mate.

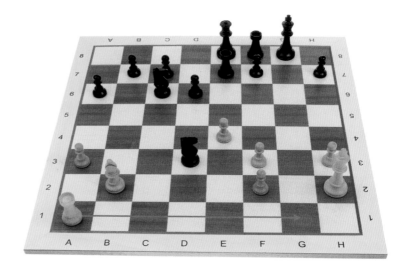

Domiano's Mate

Pedro Domiano discovered this checkmate in 1512. In this spectacular checkmate, white will sacrifice one or two Rooks to clear the way for a Queen check on the h-file and then checkmate on h7.

Domiano's Mate at a Glance

In this position, neither King can move. If it were black's move, 1.Qa7-a2 would be checkmate. White must therefore act quickly and decisively. The white pawn on g6, like the black pawn on b3, is playing a key role. The g6-pawn controls both f7 and h7. If white could find a way to place the Qc1 on h7, the game would be over.

1.Rh1-h8+ Kg8xh8
The Rook sacrifice here brings the King to the h8-square and opens up the h1-square for the Queen. Black has no choice but to capture the Rook and place the King in jeopardy on h8.

2.Qc1-h1+ Kh8-g8
With the black King exposed on h8, the white Queen gains access with check to the h-file and especially to the key h7-square. The black King has only one move, to retreat to the g8-square.

3.Qh1-h7 Checkmate

Another nice finish. White finishes the game by moving the Queen to the key h7-square. The Qh7, defended by the pawn on g6, checkmates the black King.

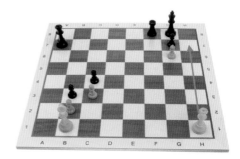

Domiano's Mate in Action

Once you have visualized these patterns, you will begin to recognize them in more complex situations. In this position, both sides have raging attacks. Black is threatening to checkmate in one move with Ra7xa2. White, however, recognizes the possibilities for a Domiano checkmate.

1.Nh4-g6+ h7xg6

White begins with a surprising Knight fork of the black King and Queen. Black could decline the sacrifice with Kh8-g8, but white would then capture the black Queen with check and next prevent the checkmate on a2 by playing a2-a3. Black opts to play h7xg6 to eliminate the Knight fork.

2.h5xg6+ Kh8-g8

White continues with an important discovered check, playing h5xg6+. The pawn capture on g6 brings check from the Rh1. Black has no choice but to retreat to g8.

CONTINUED ON NEXT PAGE

3.Rh1-h8+ Kg8xh8

As you can see, Domiano's checkmate sometimes involves the sacrifice of more than one Rook. White responds with the sacrifice of the first Rook on h8. Black is forced to recapture.

4.Rd1-h1+ Kh8-g8

The pattern repeats. White "reloads the gun" with Rd1-h1+. The idea is to sacrifice a second Rook on h8. The black King is yet again forced to retreat to g8.

5.Rh1-h8+ Kg8xh8

The second Rook sacrifice brings the King for the final time to h8. The white Queen finally has access to the h1-square, where it can deliver the key check and gain entry to the h7 mating square.

6.Qc1-h1+ Kh8-g8

White is finally able to bring the Queen with check to the h-file, where, with support from white's g6-pawn, it will have access to the key h7-square. Black retreats again to g8.

7.Qh1-h7+ Kg8-f8

As you can see, Qh1-h7+ is not quite checkmate because the black King has one final retreat to f8. In this case, the final mate resembles a back rank mate in which the black Qe7 blocks one of the escape squares.

8.Qh7-h8 Checkmate

With the final move Qh7-h8, it's checkmate.

Legal's mate usually only occurs against beginners in the opening. Black has already broken several rules in this position. The Bg4 developed before the Knights, and black has moved three pawns while leaving seven pieces "in the box." White is able to punish black's poor development with a spectacular sacrifice.

Legal's Mate in Action

1.Nf3xe5 Bg4xd1

White begins by breaking the pin from the Bg4. Black is not obligated to capture the Queen, although most beginners would. By simply recapturing the Ne5 with its d6-pawn instead, black would only be down a pawn after white's anticipated next move of 2.Qd1xg4. But black opts to capture the Queen.

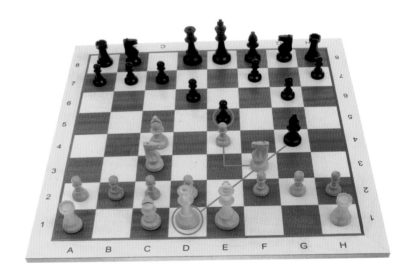

2.Bc4xf7+ Ke8-e7

Although down a Queen, white has a mate in two moves! White continues with the pawn capture on f7, check, taking advantage of the centralized Knight on e5, which now defends the f7-Bishop. The King has only one legal move, to e7.

3.Nc3-d5 Checkmate

In the final position, the white pieces harmoniously cooperate to cover all of the King's possible moves. The Nc3-d5 delivers the checkmate by attacking the King and by covering the f6 escape square. The Ne5 covers d7 and f7, while the Bf7 covers e8 and e6. It's checkmate!

FAQ

How does someone become a "master"?

By playing in a tournament, you will earn a rating. Every time you play, you will gain or lose points depending on your results and the strength of your opponent. If you defeat a strong player, you will win as many as 32 points. If you lose to a strong player, you could lose only 1 point. Of course, if you lose to a low-rated player, you could lose as many as 32 points.

The U.S. Chess Federation maintains a classification system that contains eight classes, identified by accumulated tournament points (see table at right).

If you are new to tournaments, you will begin as an unrated player and soon thereafter gain a provisional rating for your first 20 games. All of your results will count, and your first established rating will reflect those results. The ratings are used to rank players in order to make fair pairings in the events.

Points	Class
2400+	Senior Master (includes international masters and grandmasters)
2200–2399	Masters
2000–2199	Experts
1800–1999	Class A
1600–1799	Class B
1400–1599	Class C
1200–1399	Class D
0–1199	Class E

chapter 14

Attacking Themes and Common Sacrifices

Middlegame attacks are often the most exciting phase of the chess game. In this chapter, you will be able to review a number of different strategic themes for attacking an opponent. By playing through these patterns, you will be able to recognize such possibilities in your own game—either to bring them about or, if you are being attacked, to be able to prevent them. Just as important, you should be able to get a sense that successful attacks require careful coordination among many pieces, not just one or two.

Sacrifices are special kinds of attacks in which one player gives up or "sacrifices" material, perhaps as little as a pawn or as much as a Queen, in order to generate an attack. This chapter will review a number of common sacrifices that can occur in your own games.

In almost every case, attacks and sacrifices occur because one player is better developed than the other. For example, you might be able to mobilize many pieces around your opponent's King. Or perhaps if you remove one of the key defensive pieces, even at a high price, it will open direct lines against your opponent's King.

As attacks develop, you will often see that a King, as checkmate approaches, has no moves. As a general rule, when your opponent's King can't move, all you need is check! Many strong players use this rule. When you reach positions in which the opponent's King can't move, know that you can safely sacrifice material if you can find a way to deliver the final checkmate.

The Dragon Variation

The Dragon variation of the Sicilian Defense gets its name from its pawn structure. The eye of the dragon is on g7. The a6- and b7-pawns form the tail.

Notice first that black is likely to have a fianchettoed Bishop on g7, and black will be castling on the Kingside. Having moved the g-pawn from g7 to g6, the f6 and especially the h6-square have become weak. White should therefore coordinate an attack on the dark squares on the Kingside.

Slaying the Dragon

Here is a typical Dragon position. Notice that white has castled on the Queenside in order to use both Rooks in the Kingside attack. The white Be3 and the Qd2 are both pointed aggressively toward the weak h6-square. The white pawn on f3 discourages black from moving its e5-Knight to g4, where the Knight might attack the Be3 and help defend the h6-square. The f3-pawn also supports the g4-pawn. Note too that white has taken the useful precaution of moving the King from c1 to b1. It's good advice to safeguard your King from possible checks before you commence an attack.

In this position, white has at least two excellent options. There is Be3-h6, seeking to exchange the dark-squared Bishops and leaving the black King without a key defender. White could also play h2-h4, rushing the h-pawn forward toward h5 in an effort to pry open the h-file for use by the Rh1 and a Queen after Qd2-h2.

In this position, one move later, white has begun the attack with Be3-h6 while Black, eager to counterattack, has played b7-b5.

White now presses forward with h2-h4, threatening to push the h-pawn forward again to h5. Notice the usefulness of playing g2-g4 first. The pawn on g4 discouraged black from trying to defend with h7-h5.

Black has a terrible choice to make. If black captures the Bishop on h6, the white Queen will recapture and lead the attack on h6. If black declines to capture on h6, white will be able to capture on g7, which forces the black King to recapture on g7.

Again, a move later, the exchange of Bishops has occurred on g7. Black is seeking some counterplay on the Queenside with Qd8-a5. White will now continue the attack with h4-h5. The idea, of course, is to open up the h-file with h5xg6 and then with Qd2-h6 check. These attacks are very powerful and fun to play.

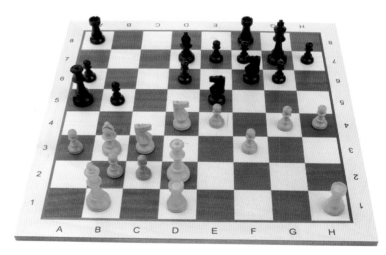

The English Attack

The attack against the Dragon works well even when black does not fianchetto the Bishop at g7. White's pawn structure against the Dragon has become known as the English attack, named after a number of English grandmasters who helped popularize the attack nearly two decades ago.

The English attack is a potent weapon for you to consider whether or not your opponent fianchettos.

An Active Kingside Attack

ONE WAY TO GO

In this position, black has again chosen to castle on the Kingside, but this time the Bf8 has developed to e7. Black's Kingside is much more secure because black has avoided the Kingside fianchetto. Nonetheless, white continues as before. White has successfully developed most of its pieces, with the Be3 and Qd2 powerfully pointing toward the Kingside. Once again, the pawn on f3 prevents Nf6-g4 and supports the beginning of an attack with g2-g4-g5.

After you have completed or nearly completed your development, you will need to make a decision about the nature of your attack. Will the attack be led by your pawns or by your pieces? That interesting decision gets easier with experience. In this position, white will lead the charge with the g-pawn, playing g2-g4. The idea is to push the pawn to g5, where the g-pawn will attack the Nf6 and force this key defender of the black Kingside to move away.

In the second figure, two moves later, white has proceeded quickly to advance the g-pawn to g5. Black has countered with b7-b5 with the idea of b5-b4 attacking the white Nc3. Black has an awkward choice in this position. The black Nf6 could retreat to e8 or move to the dim rim at h5.

Note: *As you learned in Chapter 4, "Knight Strategy," if you place a Knight on the side of the board, it will have access to only four squares. Keeping a Knight near the center yields more square access. Thus the saying, "A Knight on the rim is dim."*

Let's examine both possibilities.

Here, two moves later, black has moved the Bc8-b7, while white has "swung" the Nc3-e2 and then on to g3, where it attacks the undefended Nh5. Black dare not defend the Knight with g7-g6 because, after Ng3xh5, the resulting pawn recapture would drastically weaken the black Kingside. If, instead, black captures the Ng3, white will recapture with the h2-pawn, opening up the h-file for a forceful attack.

Here is the culmination of white's idea. After the recapture on g3 with the h2-pawn, white has played Qd2-h2 with the powerful threat of Qxh7 checkmate. Black can stop the checkmate by advancing the h-pawn, but that additional Kingside weakness will leave white with an enormous edge and an easy way to continue the attack with g5xh6.

CONTINUED ON NEXT PAGE

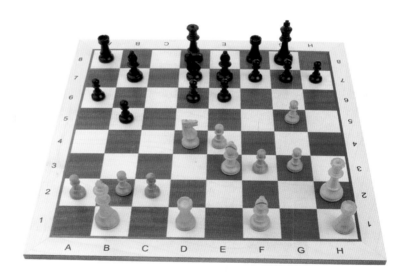

The English Attack (continued)

ANOTHER WAY

Here is a position that might have occurred had black retreated the Nf6-e8 rather than play Nf6-h5. Note that white has advanced the h2-pawn to h5. The h-pawn was needed on h2 in the event that white had to play Nc3-e2-g3. Here, the black Knight is on e8 rather than h5. White has therefore rushed the h-pawn to h5, where it can support the additional pawn advance, g5-g6.

White's strategy is becoming clear. Black will not be able to use the f7-pawn to capture on g6 because the f7-pawn is required to defend against the threat Nd4xe6 forking the Qd8 and the Rf8. Black can prevent the advance of the white g-pawn by playing g7-g6, but that move would weaken the f6 and h6 squares and permit white to open the h-file for its Rook and Queen with h5xg6. In both of these English attack examples, white opens up the h-file for an attack from the heavy pieces, the Rooks and the Queen.

TIP

What to Expect in a Tournament

When playing in a tournament, come prepared. Be sure to bring a chessboard, a chess set, and a chess clock to the events, although there are usually extras if you forget. If you need to buy equipment, the U.S. Chess Federation is a good source for the standard equipment used at most tournaments.

Chess clocks are used to allocate time fairly. Chess clocks are actually two timers in one. When you make a move, your clock stops ticking and your opponent's clock starts up. In national events, players typically must make 40 moves in 2 hours or 30 moves in 90 minutes. In local clubs, faster time limits are the norm. Often, each player gets 30 or 60 minutes for the whole game.

If you fail to make the required number of moves in the time allotted, you lose. Most of the time, however, players become nervous about the clock and speed up their play. The best advice is to play patiently and slowly. A bad move brought on by concern about the clock could permanently spoil your game.

Common Knight Sacrifices

In the opening, when you employ a gambit to sacrifice a pawn, you might expect in return to control an open file or gain an active square or two for your pieces. When you sacrifice a Knight, a Bishop, or more, you usually can expect much more compensation. In this section, two Knight sacrifices lead either to material gain or to the gain of significant positional advantages. As you observe these positions, consider how much fun it must be to offer the material, knowing the reward that may await you.

The Fried Liver Attack

In addition to having an amusing name, this opening variation provides a quick attack that many players enjoy. The moves 1.e2-e4 e7-e5, 2.Ng1-f3 Nb8-c6, and 3.Bf1-c4 Ng8-f6 are the starting position of what's called the Two Knights' Defense. This position, although only three moves into the game, permits white to try the interesting Nf3-g5 move. The Knight move breaks an important principle of moving a piece twice so early in the game, but it carries the powerful threat of Ng5xf7. To prevent the threat, black usually plays d7-d5, blocking the Bc4's attack on the f7-square.

White continues by capturing on d5 with the e4-pawn. Experienced players know that black's best response in this position would be to play Nc6-a5, threatening the white Bc4. Instead, black responds with the obvious recapture, Nf6xd5.

CONTINUED ON NEXT PAGE

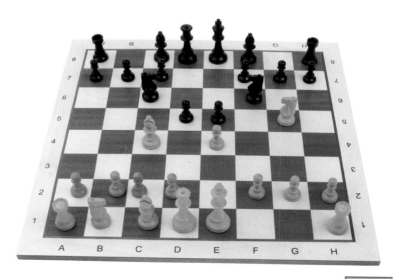

Common Knight Sacrifices (continued)

Here is the critical position. For the moment, white has only one attack on the black Nd5 with Bc4, and black has a single defender—Qd8. The Fried Liver Attack begins now with the surprising move Ng5xf7, forking the Qd8 and the Rh8. To prevent the capture of the Queen or the Rook, black must recapture the Knight with Ke8xf7.

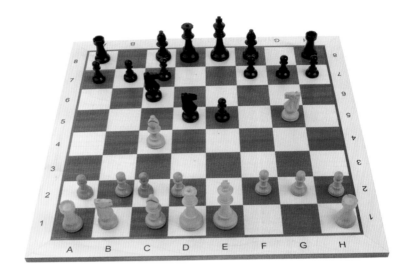

Why would white give up a Knight in this manner? In this case, because white is able to develop very quickly and force the black King into the middle of the board. First, white is able now to play Qd1-f3 check. The Queen move develops the Queen powerfully to f3 where, in addition to the check, it adds a second attack on the black Nd5. To defend the Nd5, black must bring the King farther into the center with Kf7-e6. As you might imagine, few players enjoy having their King exposed so early in the game.

White now has two attacks on the black Nd5, while black has two defenders, the Qd8 and the Ke6. Rather than capture the Nd5, white increases the pressure on the pinned Nd5 by developing the other Knight with Nb1-c3. Now facing three attacks on it's d5-Knight, black plays Nc6-b4, using the Nb4 to provide a third defense and simultaneously to threaten Nb4xc2 check, forking the white Ke1 and the Ra1.

White now has two interesting options: play Qf3-e4, defending the c2-pawn, or threaten to develop quickly with a2-a3. White plays the amazing a2-a3, attacking the black Nb4 and forcing it to carry out its threat of capturing on c2.

CONTINUED ON NEXT PAGE

Having already sacrificed a Knight, white sacrifices an additional Rook. But consider that the Ra1 has not yet moved, while black's Knight on c2 will have moved four times if it proceeds with Nc2xa1. In this position, white's King, in check, moves to d1 to force the Nc2 to move and to open the e1-square for Rh1-e1. With the Knight under attack, black naturally captures the Ra1.

White is down considerable material, but note that white now has three attacks on the black Nd5 while black has only two defenders. In compensation for the sacrifice of a Knight and a Rook, white is now able to capture the Nd5 and continue to attack with moves like Rh1-e1 and d2-d4.

Are the sacrifices correct? That question has haunted chess players for more than 400 years. Many books have been written on this subject, and still the answer is not yet clear. What *is* clear is that this type of sacrificial play is very exciting and a joy to play. By all means try to prove the soundness of the sacrifice. Or join the many players who are convinced that the Fried Liver is unsound. Either way, you will have become yet another chess player with an opinion about this exciting line.

Another Knight Sacrifice on f7

In the Caro-Kann Defense, after the moves
1.e2-e4 c7-c6, 2.d2-d4 d7-d5, 3.Nb1-d2
d5xe4, 4.Nd2xe4 Nb8-d7, 5.Bf1-c4 Ng8-f6,
6.Ne4-g5 e7-e6, 7.Qd1-e2 Bf8-e7, we reach
this position. White's Ng5, Bc4, and Qe2 are
all aiming at the e6-square. If it were black's
move, black would likely castle, moving the
King to safety. For the moment, however,
the King is the only black piece defending the
key f7-pawn, and white has an opportunity
to expose the King to a terrific attack. White
begins with the Knight sacrifice Ng5xf7. Faced
with the Knight fork of the Qd8 and the Rh8,
black recaptures with Ke8xf7.

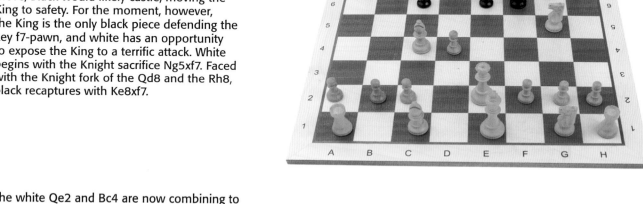

The white Qe2 and Bc4 are now combining to
attack the e6-pawn, which black is defended
only with the Kf7. White continues with the
powerful Qe2xe6 check. The black King dare
not retreat to f8 to face a Qe6-f7 checkmate.
Black therefore moves the King forward to g6.

CONTINUED ON NEXT PAGE

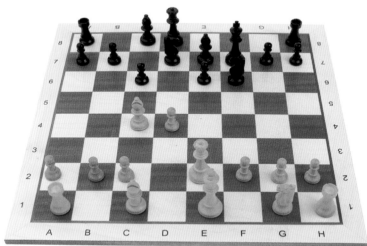

Black is clearly in trouble. There are several excellent moves here. The most efficient is Bc4-d3 check. Black's only legal response is Kg6-h5.

The end comes very quickly with Qe6-h3 checkmate. Note how well the two white Bishops control the black King's many possible escape squares.

Bishop sacrifices, like Knight sacrifices, should lead either to a significant attack or later material gain. For example, the Greco sacrifice of the Bishop on h7 leads to a complex position in which white delivers checkmate in every line. The complications can be difficult to calculate, but I hope you will begin to recognize positions in which the sacrifice could work.

The Greco Bishop Sacrifice

White begins straight away with Bd3xh7. Black is not required to recapture the Bh7, but avoiding the recapture simply permits white to win the h7-pawn. Few players will decline the offer. If black were to play Kg8-h8, white would simply continue with Nf3-g5 and then Qd1-h5 for a powerful attack.

Black opted to recapture with Kg8xh7; white has given up a Bishop. In compensation for the material, the black King is now exposed. White's plan is to play Nf3-g5 and, if the black King retreats, follow up with Qd1-h5 and then the Qh5-h7 checkmate.

CONTINUED ON NEXT PAGE

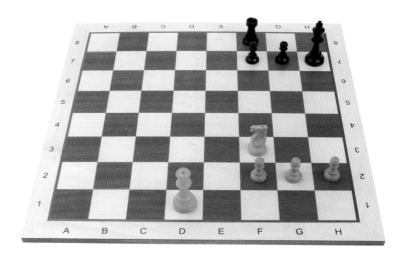

GRECO'S SACRIFICE IN ACTION

Many of these sacrifices work because one side has far better development than the other. This is certainly true here. White has successfully advanced the e-pawn to e5, attacking black's Nf6, which has retreated to d7. As a result, the black Knight is no longer on f6, where it can defend the Kingside, notably the h7-square.

White begins by playing with Bd3xh7 check. Only the King can recapture. Black is not required to recapture, but moving the King to h8 would lose the h7-pawn with no compensation and only invite additional moves like Nf3-g5 and Qd1-h5 for a powerful attack. Black therefore captures the Bishop with Kg8xh7.

Having sacrificed the Bishop, white should play aggressively, not permitting black time to safeguard the King. White therefore continues with Nf3-g5 check. Black dare not capture the Ng5 with the Qd8 because the white Bc1 defends the Knight. Black therefore must move the King. Black rejects the move Kh7-h8 because white would win quickly with Qd1-h5 check followed by Qh5-h7 checkmate.

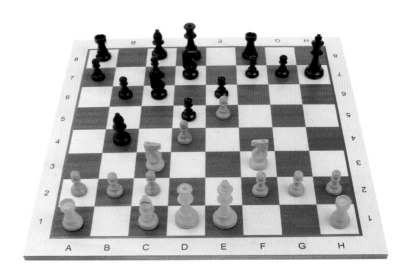

First Variation: Kh7-g8

Here, after the retreat of the black King to g8, white continues the attack with Qd1-h5, with the important threat of Qh5-h7 checkmate. Fortunately for black, the Queen's arrival on h5 is not check. To delay the checkmate, black plays Rf8-e8 to give the black King an escape to f8.

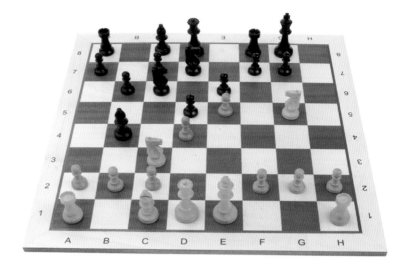

By moving off the f8-square, the black Rook no longer defends the f7-pawn. White, with two attacks on the f7-pawn, plays Qh5xf7 check, which forces the black King to retreat to h8.

CONTINUED ON NEXT PAGE

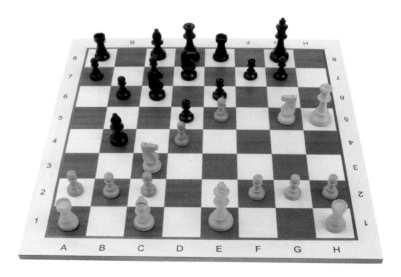

In this position, see if you can find the check-mate in four moves. The solution? The game ends quickly after the following forced sequence:

Qf7-h5+ Kh8-g8
Qh5-h7+ Kg8-f8
Qh7-h8+ Kf8-e7
Qh8xg7 checkmate

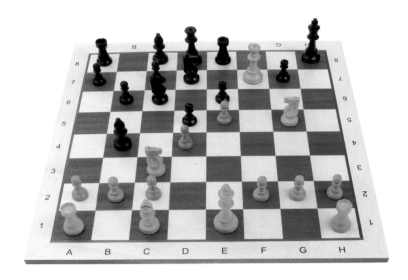

Second Variation: Kh7-h6

Now, let's see what happens if black opts to retreat the King from its check on h7 to the h6-square. The move by the black King does prevent white from moving the Queen to h5, but the Kh6 is suddenly on the c1-h6 diagonal. Any movement now by the Ng5 will be a powerful discovered check. The best of those moves is probably Ng5xe6, revealing the check from the Bishop and attacking both the black Qd8 and the Rf8. No matter what black's response, white will be able to win the black Queen—clearly wonderful compensation for the sacrificed Bishop.

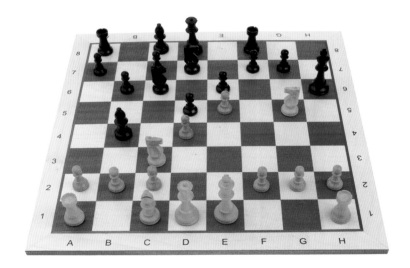

Third Variation: Kh7-g6

Finally, what if black moved Kh7-g6? In this position, the black King is dangerously exposed, but it does prevent white from playing Qd1-h5. White has two other strong ideas. White could play Qd1-g4, threatening discovered checks like Ng5xe6. Or white could play what may be an even more powerful move, h2-h4. The pawn advance would provide additional support for the Knight and threaten the h4-h5 check. The King would then have to move to the dangerous h6-square when discovered checks from an Ng5-move again become possible.

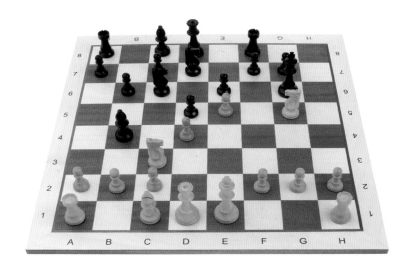

Bishop Sacrifices on h6

As you can see, black has weakened the Kingside by advancing the h-pawn to h6. If you have a lead in development, you might want to consider the following Bishop sacrifice. White begins by playing Be3xh6. Not wanting to lose the h6-pawn for no reason, black recaptures with g7xh6.

CONTINUED ON NEXT PAGE

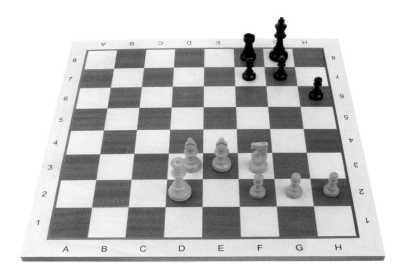

Bishop Sacrifices
(continued)

White has given up the Bishop but, as you can see, the black Kingside has been broken up as a result. Here, white can continue with Qd2xh6, with the immediate threat of Qh6-h7 checkmate and, if necessary, Nf3-g5 with the threat of Qh6-h7 mate.

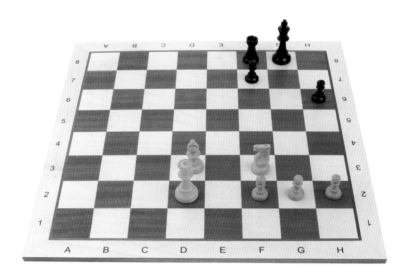

THE BXH6 SACRIFICE IN ACTION

White will begin in this position with the Bishop sacrifice on h6. You can see that the Queen will be able to follow up with Qd2xh6. The Bc2 will clearly play an important role in supporting the threat of checkmate on h7.

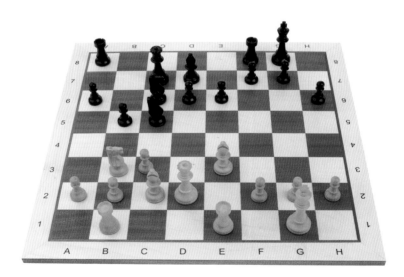

This is the position after the Bishop sacrifice on h6 and black's recapture with g7xh6. The black h6-pawn is now isolated and weak. White will continue the attack with Qd2xh6, threatening Qh6-h7 checkmate. To stop the mate, black plays the move f7-f5, blocking the Bc2's support for the mate and providing the f7-escape square for the King.

The advance of the black f-pawn has left the g6-square open for the white Queen. White plays Qh6-g6 check, forcing the black King to h8.

CONTINUED ON NEXT PAGE

The black King can't move now. To end the game, white only needs to deliver check from a piece other than the Queen. White sees that the Re1 can now move to e3 and then slide to the h-file on h3, delivering the final blow. With the Kingside in shambles and poor development, black has no way to prevent the checkmate from occurring.

A Bishop Sacrifice on f7

It is readily apparent that white has good control over the center in this position. The two center pawns are unopposed, and white's Nf3 and Bc4 are already actively placed. By contrast, black has fianchettoed the Bg7 and developed the Queen's Knight to d7. Black's last move, Nb8-d7, probably should have been Ng8-f6 to develop the Knight toward the center and to prepare for castling.

White can now take advantage of black's lack of development by playing the impressive Bc4xf7 check. Black can decline this Bishop sacrifice offer with Ke8-f8, but white would then simply be ahead a pawn with a nice attack brewing with moves such as Nf3-g5 and Qd1-f3. Black therefore accepts the sacrifice with Ke8xf7.

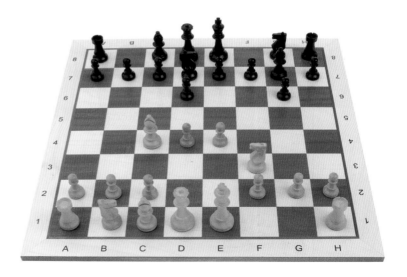

White is down material in this position, but there is significant compensation. Black's King is exposed to attack, and white has the development to take advantage of black's weaknesses. White plays Nf3-g5 check. In response, the black King has three choices. Retreating to e8 or f8 loses the Queen immediately after Ng5-e6! Black therefore decides to play it's only other option, Kf7-f6.

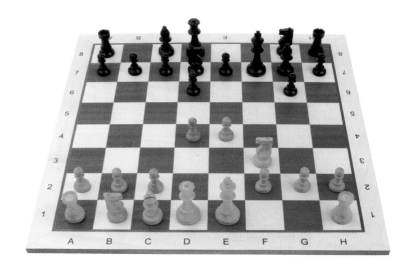

Note that the black King can't move now. White therefore plays Qd1-f3 checkmate.

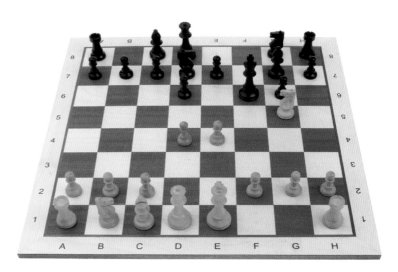

Exchange Sacrifices

An exchange sacrifice, or "the sacrifice of the exchange," occurs when one player exchanges a Rook for a "minor piece," either a Knight or a Bishop. This section introduces two common exchange sacrifices, one for white and one for black. The themes should be familiar to you. As compensation for the lost material, the player giving up the Rook for the minor piece gains open files against the opponent's King and active squares for the remaining pieces.

An Exchange Sacrifice on h5

In the Dragon variation, to break through to the King, white often must sacrifice a Rook for a Knight. For example, in this position, white would like to checkmate quickly with Qh6xh7, but the black Nf6 is defending the h7-square. White therefore begins by advancing the g4-pawn to g5, kicking the Nf6. The Knight must move or be captured. Black therefore plays Nf6-h5, blocking the h-file and continuing to prevent white from checkmating on h7.

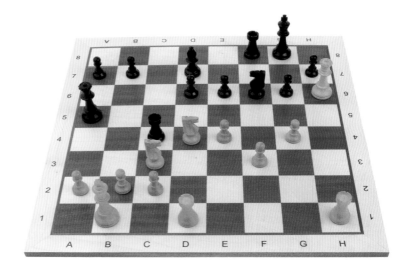

To break through to the King, white continues the attack with an exchange sacrifice, Rh1xh5. Obviously, the move offers the Rh1 for the Nh5, but it succeeds in breaking up the black Kingside and setting up the final checkmate. Faced with the threat of Qh6xh7 and needing compensation for the loss of the Knight, black recaptures with g6xh5.

With the g6-pawn gone, white is now able to continue the attack with g5-g6. The pawn move permits white to threaten Qh6xh7 checkmate. Black could defend against the checkmate by sacrificing the Rf8 on f7, but after g6xf7 check, white would have a significant material advantage. Instead, black captures the pawn on g6 with h7xg6.

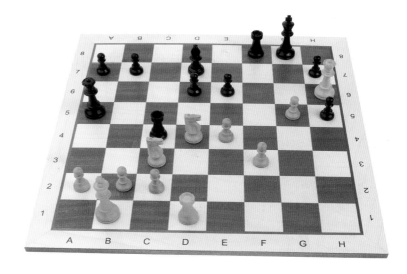

The end is near. Having broken though, white continues with Qh6xg6 check, which forces the black King into the corner.

CONTINUED ON NEXT PAGE

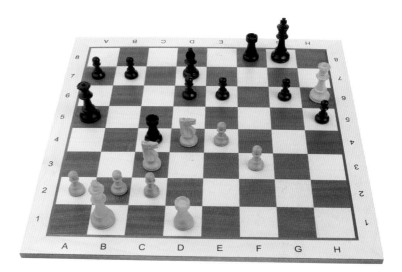

Exchange Sacrifices
(continued)

There are many ways for white to finish the game quickly. The most accurate is the move Rd1-g1, with the threats of Qg6-g7 checkmate, as well as Qg6-h6 checkmate and even Qg6xh5 checkmate. To delay the checkmates, black could sacrifice the Qa5 on a2, but most players with the black pieces would probably resign after Rd1-g1.

An Exchange Sacrifice on c3

Not all sacrifices and victories in the Dragon variation are played by white. Here is a typical exchange sacrifice that will help the player with the black pieces gain a victory or two.

In this position, white has begun an attack on the black Kingside with h2-h4-h5 and with Be3-h6. Black has responded by posting the Queen aggressively on a5 and by doubling the Rooks on the c-file. Note that black would like to play Qa5xa2, but the white Nc3 is defending the a-pawn. Black therefore begins with Rc7xc3, an exchange sacrifice that removes a key defender. White could ignore the capture with a move like Bh6xg7, but white decides instead to accept the exchange sacrifice with b2xc3.

As you can see, the sacrifice of the exchange has resulted in severe damage to the pawns around the white King. The c-pawns are doubled. Black has two attacks on the c3-pawn, which is defended only by the white Queen. Rather than capture the c3-pawn, black decides instead to play Qa5xa2 with the powerful threat Qa2-a1 checkmate. In an effort to guard the a1-square and prevent the immediate checkmate, white responds with Nd4-b3.

Black would like to continue with Rc8xc3, but the white Queen on d2 is guarding the c3-pawn. Black therefore plays Bg7xh6, attacking the Qd2 and forcing white to respond with Qd2xh6, a move that white usually likes to play, but here it removes the Queen from its role in defending the Queenside pawns.

CONTINUED ON NEXT PAGE

With the white Queen now on h6, black can continue the attack with Rc8xc3, a capture that carries the threat of Rc3xc2 checkmate as well as Qa2xc2 checkmate. Seeing that after Rd1-d2, black could simply play Qa2xb3 (taking advantage of the fact that Rc3 pins the white c2-pawn), white responds instead with Nb3-d4, using the Nd4 to defend the c2-pawn.

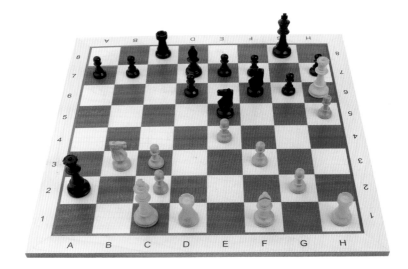

Already with firm control over the white Queenside, black now offers a Knight sacrifice with Ne5-g4, attacking the white Queen. With no good retreats for the white Queen (Qh6-g5 meets Rc3-c5, Qh6-f4 meets e7-e5, and Qh6-d2 meets Qa2-a1 checkmate), white captures the black Knight with f3xg4.

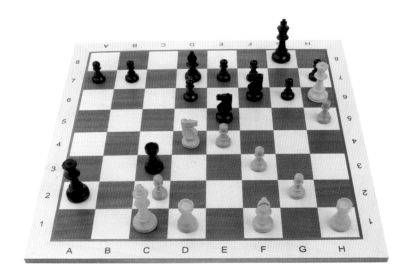

Black now plays Nf6xe4, capturing a central white pawn but, more important, taking control over the key d2-square that the white King needs for its escape. White is now helpless. The white Queen can sacrifice itself to delay checkmate, but the threat of Qa2-a1 is simply too difficult to stop. If Nd4-b3, for example, black would immediately end the game with Qa2xc2 checkmate.

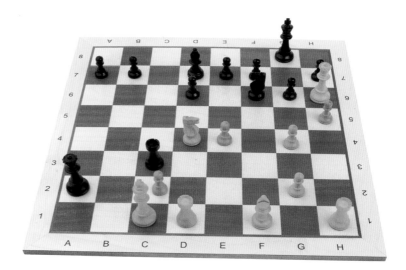

FAQ

Are there different types of chess tournaments?

Yes. The most common type of chess tournament in the United States is the Swiss tourney or Swiss system. In these tournaments, players who win are paired against other winners. And so, the final round often consists of two undefeated players competing for first place. If you lose several games in a Swiss system, your next pairing is likely to get easier. By using a Swiss system, tournaments need only four to six rounds and can take place within a two-day weekend.

Major championships tend to be round-robins, in which each player plays every other player in the field. Such events tend to take place over a week or longer.

chapter **15**

An Introduction to Endgames

If both sides have played with reasonable care, the result at the end of the game is often what appears at first to be a very simple position. There are just one or two pieces on the board and perhaps just a handful of pawns. As you will see in this chapter, it is possible to gain victory with just a small advantage. You will learn how to win with an extra pawn, and hopefully, how to draw if you are down a pawn.

The strategies in this chapter are relatively straightforward, but they form a solid foundation for your middlegame strategy. Perhaps you will be able to exchange pieces to reach a position similar to one in this chapter. Transitions to favorable endgames are at the heart of a master's strategy. Many beginning players prefer to spend their time learning opening variations. Strong players often begin at the end, mastering the subtleties of these endgames in the expectation that their opponents will not know what to do in this phase of the game.

No one will expect that you will study endgames for years, but having knowledge of the positions in this chapter will help you to play your endgames with much more confidence. Throughout this chapter, you'll also find helpful sidebars highlighting basic endgame principles that you need to keep in mind as you play and learn.

King and pawn endgames seem simple but can be quite complex. This section will focus on several key positions that you are likely to experience. Some involve offense, trying to Queen a single remaining pawn. Others involve defense, trying to prevent your opponent from promoting a pawn to a Queen. Mastery of these simple positions will greatly aid your game.

The Strategy

THE MAGIC POSITION

This first position is worth remembering because, no matter whose move it is, white will successfully be able to promote the pawn. As you can see, the white King is in front of the pawn. That's the key! In this position, if it is black's move, the black King must move to either d8 or to f8. Either way, the poor King must leave the square on which the white pawn will be promoted. White will then be able to move the King forward to gain control over the Queening square.

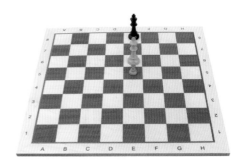

In this position, after just one move, the situation has become completely clear. White has complete control over the key e8-square as well as the e6 and e7 squares through which the white pawn will now travel. White will successfully promote the pawn into a Queen and then proceed with a King and Queen to deliver the checkmate we reviewed in Chapter 12, "Elementary Checkmates."

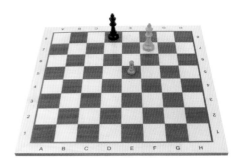

That was easy, but what if white has to move first from the Magic position. It's still a win for white. From this same position, white begins by sliding the King to d6 or f6, making way to push the pawn forward. Whichever direction the white King selects, black will move in the same direction, attempting to prevent the white King from moving forward and capturing easy control over the e8-Queening square.

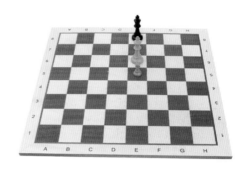

Having made room for the advance of the pawn, white pushes it forward. Black has no choice but to defend the Queening square by occupying it.

Now, white again pushes the e6-pawn to e7. Note the key principle. The pawn advances WITHOUT giving check to the black King. The King has only one legal move, Ke8-f7.

CONTINUED ON NEXT PAGE

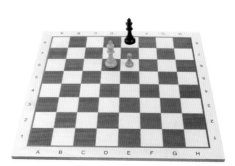

White has a choice, but only one correct move. Queening the pawn would be a significant error because the black Kf7 would simply capture it! The key move is to patiently move the white King to d7 where it controls the Queening square and prepares the successful advance of the pawn to e8.

HOW TO STOP THE PAWN?

Here, with black on the defense, black must simply prevent the white King from moving in front of its pawn. Black therefore moves Ke7-d7, placing itself opposite the white King. Chess players call this "taking the opposition."

White now advances the pawn with e6 check. The black King, whenever it can, should occupy the square directly in front of the pawn.

White can't move the pawn because the black King is blocking its path. Therefore, white must move the King. With Kd5-e5, white defends its pawn. Whenever the black King must move from the square in front of the pawn, it needs to move directly backwards.

Here's the key. If white advances the King to either d6 or f6, black must take the opposition. On Ke5-d6, black must play King to d8. If instead, white plays Ke5-f6, black must move its King to f8.

Now, when white advances the pawn to e7, it is with a check. The black King moves to block the advance of the pawn with Kd8-e8.

CONTINUED ON NEXT PAGE

In this final position, white has a terrible choice. Kd6-e6 is a stalemate, a draw, and all other moves permit black to capture the pawn.

THE RULE OF THE SQUARE

To make it simpler to calculate long sequences, chess players have introduced a counting tool called "the Rule of the Square."

In this position, the white pawn is moving toward the h8-Queening square. You can see that the white h-pawn needs just three more moves to reach the h8-Queening square, while the black King needs four moves to reach h8. To make it simpler to see if the King can capture the pawn, imagine that the white pawn forms a four by four square. The highlighted area forms a square in which each length is the distance that the pawn must travel in order to become a Queen. The key principle is that the defending black King must be able to enter that highlighted area in order to be able to capture the pawn successfully. With black to move, the black King easily moves into the highlighted region by playing Kd4-e5.

If, however, it were white's move, h5-h6 would reduce the size of the highlighted area, and the black King would not be able to reach it in time.

Exceptions to the Rule

Most rules have exceptions. Here are two special cases. This is the same diagram as above, but with the addition of a black pawn on f6. The black King can enter the square of the white pawn but will not be able to do so again as the white pawn advances. The reason, of course, is that the black pawn on f6 is blocking the black King's path toward the h8-Queening square.

Here is a second exception. It certainly appears at first glance that the black King will be able to reach the white pawn. The square is larger, and after white moves h2-h3, the black King would indeed be able to reach the pawn in time. However, white can begin with h2-h4! Suddenly, by moving ahead two squares, the black King will be unable to reach the pawn.

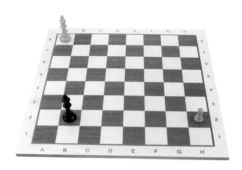

THE POWER OF THE OPPOSITION

You have already seen that using the opposition can help you to draw against a King and a pawn. The opposition can also help you to win. In this position, white could try to advance the h-pawn quickly, but after h2-h4 black would be able to enter the square of the pawn with Kd3-e4 and eventually capture it.

Rather than advance the h-pawn directly, white should instead take the opposition with Kc5-d5, blocking the black King's access to the e4-square. Black will therefore continue with Kd3-e3 in an effort to reach the white h-pawn.

White could now advance the h-pawn with h2-h4, but again the black King would be able to enter the square of the pawn after Ke3-f4. Showing off the power of the opposition, white again continues with Kd5-e5 and black continues to move toward the pawn with Ke3-f3.

CONTINUED ON NEXT PAGE

The opposition pays off this time with Ke5-f5 because the black King cannot move to the g3-square. Black therefore tries to reach the h2-pawn with Kf3-g2, an act of some desperation.

The finale is now clear. White simply plays h2-h4 and the black King will not be able to capture it. The h-pawn will race unimpeded down the board and promote on the h8-Queening square.

SELF-SUPPORTING PAWNS

Late in the game, the pawns are often capable of defending themselves from capture. In this position for example, the King can capture the white pawn on d4, but the capture would bring the King outside the square of the c5-pawn. These pawns are therefore said to be "self-supporting."

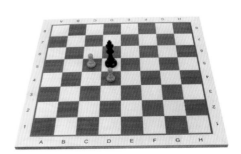

It might surprise you, but these two pawns are also self-supporting. Black can move the King in an attempt to capture one of them, but white will respond simply by advancing the other pawn. For example, black might play the move Kd6-e5, attacking the white e4-pawn. White would respond with c4-c5.

It is clear that black dare not capture the e4-pawn here because that capture would bring the King outside the square of the c5-pawn. White would simply advance the c5-pawn to c6 and soon thereafter promote the c-pawn to a Queen.

TIP

Basic Endgame Principle #1: Stay Active

The most important end game principle is to stay active. Often, in response to threats, beginners tend to defend against those threats rather than to counter-attack with threats of their own. Stay active, and think about responding with a threat of your own.

Endgames that involve only Rooks and pawns are the most common type of endgames between strong players. These endgames are quite challenging, but having a firm understanding of the three main positions here will help you to survive the complexities. Remember, keep your Rooks active, even if doing so requires that you consider giving up a pawn. The player with the most active Rook and King will almost always win these endgames.

TWO CONNECTED PASSED PAWNS VS. A ROOK

This first position illustrates that two connected passed pawns on the 6th rank are more powerful than a Rook. Even with black to move, there's simply no way to prevent at least one of the pawns from successfully promoting to a Queen. Black's best hope might be to attack one of the pawns from the rear, but white will respond by advancing the pawn that is not attacked.

Black could now capture the c6-pawn, but white would successfully promote the other pawn. Instead, white could move the Rook behind the more advanced d-pawn. Of course, white would respond by advancing the c-pawn.

It's clear in this position that one of the pawns will Queen. The back Rook can capture the d-pawn, but there's simply no way for the Rook to capture both pawns.

THE SECRET TO REACHING A DRAW

In the section on King and pawn endgames, you learned that to win, the winning side needs to place its King in front of its advancing pawn. The same holds true here. In this position, white is threatening to play Ke5-e6. Black could try to check the white King with Ra2-e2, but the white King could escape check by moving in front of the pawn on d6. Similarly, after Ke5-e6, black could check the King with Ra2-a6. But white would simply advance the pawn to d6, with the terrible threat of Rb1-b8 checkmate!

With black to move, in order to draw, black must play Ra2-a6 to prevent the white King from moving in front of its pawn. White can move the Rook around for a while, but so long as black's Rook maintains control over the 6th rank, the white King will not be able to move in front of its pawn. To make progress, white will therefore have to advance the d5-pawn to d6.

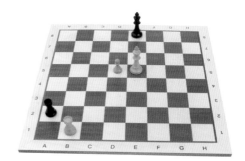

As soon as white advances the d-pawn, black must move the Rook back as far as safely possible to the 1st or 2nd rank, in this case, back to a2. White can play Ke5-e6, threatening checkmate with Rb1-b8, but black will be able to draw.

CONTINUED ON NEXT PAGE

Although the threat of checkmate with Rb1-b8 is in the air, black has a simple draw. Rather than Ra2-a8 to defend the checkmate, black decides to check the white King with Ra2-e2. Note that, with the pawn on d6, there's simply no place for white to escape a never ending series of checks. If white decides to approach the black Rook with the King, black will be able to approach and then capture the d6-pawn with Ke8-d7.

WINNING WITH THE EXTRA PAWN

The major difference between this position and the last is that the white King already controls the Queening square on e8. Note, however, that the white King cannot legally move off to one side and then Queen the pawn. For the moment at least, the white King cannot move because the black King defends d8 and d7, and the black Rook defends f8 and f7.

In order to win, white must drive back the black King and then find a clever way to shield the white King from attacks by the black Rook. White begins by playing Rh2-c2 check, forcing the black King to retreat to the b-file.

In order to construct a shield of protection for the white King, white plays the impressive move Rc2-c4. The purpose of this Rook move might not be immediately apparent. I recommend that you review this small section at least twice in order to understand the importance of this move. The Rc4 will, after several more moves, help to erect a shield in the center with the white King on e5 and the Rook protecting against checks on the e4-square. Chess players call this "building a bridge." Black responds to white's Rc2-c4 by moving its King to b6, hoping to advance to b5 to attack the c4-Rook.

White is now ready to try to promote the e-pawn by playing Ke8-d7. As you can see, after the King leaves the e8-Queening square, white threatens to promote the e-pawn to a Queen. Black must therefore check the King with the Rook (Rf1-d1) in an effort to delay or prevent the pawn promotion.

There is no point in returning the King to the e8-square. Rather, white plays Kd7-e6, again threatening to promote the e-pawn. Black continues to check the white King with Rd1-e1 check.

White must be careful here. Ke6-d5, for example, would permit black simply to capture the e-pawn. White therefore prepares the construction of the shield more patiently, first with Ke6-d6. Again, black continues to check the white King by playing Re1-d1 check.

CONTINUED ON NEXT PAGE

Now, with no direct threat to the e7-pawn, white simply plays Kd6-e5, again with the threat of promoting the e7-pawn. Black must again deliver check with the Rook, this time from e1.

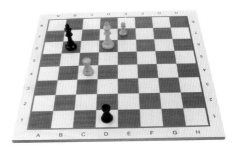

White's strategy has finally paid off. In this position, white simply blocks the check from the black Rook by playing Rc4-e4, the culmination of white's strategy. Black has no chances in the final position because there are no further delaying checks. Black might exchange Rooks, but the white pawn will now Queen successfully.

TIP

Basic Endgame Principle #2: Think Ahead
Beginners tend to think about each move only as it occurs rather than thinking strategically. To succeed in chess, you should think three moves ahead—try to envision your future moves, as well as your opponent's likely responses.

In simple endgames that involve only a single Bishop with an outside passed pawn, the key is often whether the Bishop can control the Queening square. In endgames that involve Bishops on both sides, you should be concerned with whether the Bishops are of the same or of opposite color. Endgames that involve Bishops of the same color usually have one good and one bad Bishop. As you might expect, a good Bishop will usually help you to win the game. When the Bishops are of opposite color—one dark-squared and one light-squared—games are often drawn.

Single Bishop and Rook Pawn Endgames

WHEN THE BISHOP CAN CONTROL THE QUEENING SQUARE

This first Bishop endgame is a very simple win because white's dark-squared Bishop is able to control the h8-Queening square. White begins by advancing the h6-pawn to h7, giving check to the black King. Black could retreat to f8, permitting the pawn to Queen, but black prefers to play Kg8-h8 to block the pawn.

Note: *A Rook pawn is defined as a pawn on either the a- or h-file. It's called a Rook pawn because Rooks start on the a- and h-files at the beginning of the game.*

As you can see, now the black King cannot move. All white needs to do is check. Bg5-f6 is a very quick checkmate, all made possible by the fact that white's dark-squared Bishop is able to control the dark h8-Queening square.

CONTINUED ON NEXT PAGE

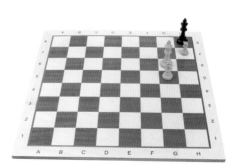

WHEN THE BISHOP CANNOT CONTROL
THE QUEENING SQUARE

It surprises many beginners, but even with a Bishop and pawn, white cannot win here. Unlike the last position, the light-squared Bishop on g4 will not be able to control the dark h8-Queening square. White again begins by pushing the h6-pawn to h7, and black gladly responds with Kg8-h8.

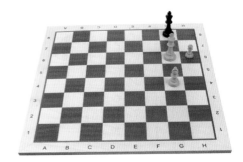

Here, the black King cannot move, but there is no way for white to deliver the final checkmate. On any Bishop move, the game will end in a stalemate. White could retreat the King, but black would then capture the pawn. Unfortunately for white here, a King and Bishop is an insufficient force to deliver checkmate.

Bishops of Opposite Color

A DRAW

In this situation, the remaining Bishops on the board each travel on different colored squares. Black's Bishop can move only on the light squares. White's Bishop can travel only on the dark squares. As such, the two Bishops will never be able to attack each other.

Endgames that involve Bishops of opposite color are so drawish (or likely to end a draw) that even with an advantage of two and sometimes even three pawns, they simply cannot be won. As you can see in this position, white is ahead in material by two pawns. However, black has assembled a firm blockade on the light squares with the Bd5 and the Ke6. White, with its dark-squared Bishop, simply cannot force the black King or the black Bishop to move off and permit the white pawns to advance. Indeed, black can simply move the Bishop back and forth between any safe light square and the d5-square. Unable to make any progress, white should offer a draw.

NOT ALL OPPOSITE-COLORED ENDGAMES ARE DRAWISH

In endgames with Bishops of opposite color, it is much easier to win when the two pawns are separated by several files because the defending side cannot easily blockade both pawns. In this position, black is blockading the white c6-pawn with the King, but that leaves only the Bg7 to prevent white from advancing and promoting the g4-pawn.

White's strategy is simple. Force the black King to commit to stopping one of the pawns and then use the white King to assist the advance of the other pawn. Here, white begins with Ke4-f5, moving toward the g6-square. Black dare not move the King too far away from the c6-pawn. Therefore, black decides to move the Bishop along the long a1-h8 diagonal to b2.

White continues with g4-g5 to bring the pawn closer to the Queening square. By later bringing the white King to either f7 or h7, the King will be able to guide the g-pawn all the way toward the g8-Queening square. Black again moves the Bishop along the long diagonal, this time to d4.

White now plays Kf5-e6, cutting off the black King's access to d6 and with the idea of Ke6-f7, guiding in the g-pawn toward the g8-square. Black, without any good play, moves the Bishop to e3 to attack the g5-pawn.

CONTINUED ON NEXT PAGE

The end is near. White reacts to the threat of Be3xg5 by advancing the pawn to g6. The rest is easy. White will continue with Ke6-f7 and then guide the g-pawn to g7. Black will probably capture the pawn on g7 with the Bishop, but after recapturing black's Bishop, white will have a very easy win. Black will only have the King left and will have to move it, unblocking the c6-pawn and allowing it to promote to a Queen. White will move its King over to assist the advance of the c6-pawn. Checkmate will be just a few moves away.

TIP

Basic Endgame Principle #3: Place Your Pieces on Active Squares

Another key principle is to consider where your pieces are best placed. In most positions, there are strong squares or *outposts* that are immune from capture by enemy pawns, and *entry squares*, undefended squares deep in your opponent's position that permit the pieces to become active and to remain active. Keeping your Knights in the center, opening files for your Rooks and Queen, and placing your Bishops on long diagonals are all good ways to get the most action from your pieces.

The Knight is usually not quite as powerful as the Bishop in the endgame. Consider, for example, that the Bishop can control a key square from a large distance, while the Knight can take a few moves to reach a key square. As you'll learn in this section, a victory for either side is possible when it's down to a Knight and a pawn.

The Strategy

A DRAW

In this first example, the black pawn is ready to promote on e1. Only the Knight can stop it. With black to move, the black King could capture the Knight and then Queen the pawn. It is white's move, however, and the Knight is able to maintain control over the Queening square.

White begins by moving the Knight to e1, blocking the advance of the pawn. Black responds by moving its King to d2, forcing the white Knight to move.

White has two adequate options here. First, Ne1-g2 would continue to guard the e1-square and also prevent the black King from moving to e3 and thereafter to f2 in order to drive off the Knight. The second option is Ne1-f3 check. This move would guard the e1-square and force the black King to move—most likely to e3 in an effort to force the Knight away from its control over the key e1-square.

CONTINUED ON NEXT PAGE

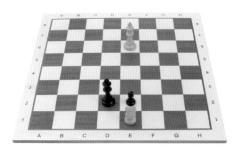

As you can see, there is simply no way to drive the Knight away. White will respond with Nf3-e1. After some patient maneuvering, both sides are likely to finally agree on a draw.

SOMETIMES THE PAWN CAN WIN!

When it is able to control a square through which a passed pawn must travel, the Knight obviously has the ability to prevent the promotion of the pawn.

However in this position, the Knight is unable to blockade the pawn. It's white's move. Because white must prevent black from capturing the h5-pawn with Ng7xh5, white advances its pawn to h6 to attack the black Knight.

There is no square that the Knight can move to that will help to prevent the pawn from reaching h8. Black instead tries to race the King toward h8 by playing Ke8-f8, and in turn, defending the Knight.

In this key position, white would make a significant error by capturing the black Knight. That would lead to an uninteresting draw after Kf8xg7. Instead, white cleverly continues to advance the pawn to h7. Notice that the pawn on h7 prevents the black King from moving to g8 where it would be closer to the h7-pawn. The Knight is also unable to prevent the h7-pawn from promoting to a Queen on h8.

A KNIGHT AND ROOK PAWN WILL ALWAYS WIN

Unlike the endgame with a Bishop and pawn when the pawn does not always promote (see pages 257–260 earlier in this chapter), the Knight will never have a problem controlling the Queening square so the pawn will always be able to promote to a Queen.

In this position, white needs only to be careful not to stalemate the black King. For example, if white pushes the h6-pawn to h7, the black King will not be in check and will not have a legal move. The result will be a stalemate, an unfortunate draw for white.

To win, white should begin by playing Ng5-f7 check to drive the black King from the Queening square to g8.

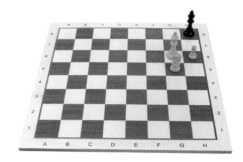

The rest is quite easy. Now that white has control over the key h8-Queening square, white pushes the pawn to h7, delivering check and forcing the King away to f8.

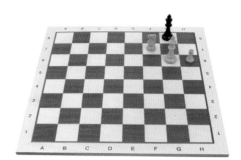

The h-pawn now Queens, forcing the King to e7.

CONTINUED ON NEXT PAGE

White has a very quick mate, in part because Queens and Knights work very well together. White proceeds by moving the new Queen from h8 to d8, check. It's a powerful move that uses the Knight on f7 to defend the Queen on d8 and forces the black King to e6.

White ends the game quickly with a beautiful checkmate, Qd8-d6#, again using the Knight on f7 to support the Queen on d6. Notice how the Knight, Queen, and King work together.

TIP

Basic Endgame Principle #4: Activate Your King

In the opening and in the middlegame, it is a good strategy to safeguard the King, often by moving it into the corner. This isn't so in the endgame. In the final phase of the game, the King becomes a powerful piece. After the Queens have been exchanged and there is no danger of a checkmate, it is often a good idea to begin moving your King forward or toward key sectors of the board. Perhaps the King will prevent an enemy piece from gaining control over a key outpost or entry square. Or perhaps the King will help to guide a passed pawn toward the Queening square. Either way, you are more likely to win in the endgame if your King is more active than your opponent's King.

Queen endgames are less common than Rook endgames. When they occur, they are even more challenging. The reason, of course, is that the Queen is an extremely powerful piece, and the player with the Queen will have many options to consider. A few simple examples in this section can help you to cope with these complexities.

The Strategy

QUEEN AGAINST A LONE ROOK PAWN

As you should expect, the Queen will almost always be able to prevent a pawn from Queening. In this example, the black pawn is only two squares away from the h1-Queening square, and the white King is too far away to provide immediate help. Nonetheless, white can win very quickly.

White begins with Qa6-g6+. Black responds with Kg1-f2, with the idea of being able to advance the pawn to h2.

There are many paths to the win here, but white decides to play Qg6-f5+ to check and, at the same time, attack the h3-pawn. The black King responds with Kf2-g3 in an effort to prevent the Queen from moving toward the black pawn.

CONTINUED ON NEXT PAGE

White presses on with Qf5-g5+. Black tries to prevent the white Queen from reaching g4 by playing Kg3-f3.

White continues to make steady progress by playing Qg5-h4. It's not check, but it does attack the undefended h-pawn. If black loses the pawn, the resulting endgame is extremely simple. Black therefore defends the h-pawn with Kf3-g2.

After white plays Qh4-g4+, the black King has no choice but to continue to defend the h-pawn with Kg2-h2.

It is white's move in this position, but white notices that, if it were black's move, black would have only one legal move—Kh2-h1. It's a move that would permit white to capture the h-pawn. White therefore can make any King move to force black to give up the h-pawn after Kh2-h1.

THE QUEEN AGAINST A MORE ADVANCED PAWN

In the previous example, the Queen was able to stop the advance of a Rook pawn on the 6th rank all by itself. Here, the pawn is in the middle of the board but more advanced. The Queen can succeed again, but this time only with help from the King.

In this position, black is ready to promote the pawn on e1. The white Queen could capture the e2-pawn, but that would lead to an immediate draw once the black King recaptured.

Instead, white wants to bring the King on d5 closer to the pawn. Therefore, white begins with Qe3-d3+, knowing that in order to continue to defend the e2-pawn, the black King will have to move to e1, thus blocking its own pawn from Queening.

Once the black King is forced to block the advance of the e-pawn, white gains the opportunity to bring the King toward the pawn. White therefore plays Kd5-e4. In an effort to mobilize the pawn, black moves Ke1-f2, again threatening to promote the e-pawn.

CONTINUED ON NEXT PAGE

Once again, white attacks the King by playing Qd3-f3+. Note that on f3, the Queen is attacking both the King and the e2-pawn. In order to continue to defend the pawn, black once again is forced to return to the e1-square, blocking the e-pawn.

Again, white takes the opportunity to advance the King, this time to the d3-square. Black can resign now, because white will now be able to capture the e2-pawn with the Queen on the next move and deliver checkmate soon thereafter.

NOT ALL QUEENS WILL CATCH THE PAWN

This position is a special case. The black h-pawn is on h2, only one square away from Queening. Unfortunately for white, the white King is far off and there is, as you will see, no way to bring the King close enough to capture the pawn. With white to move, white could simply play Qh3-f1 checkmate. However, with black to move, black will move Kh1-g1, black's only legal move.

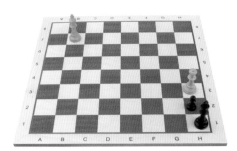

White now has a problem. Black is threatening to Queen the h-pawn. To prevent the advance of the pawn, white plays Qh3-g3+, and black happily moves the King back into the corner. As you can see, black is out of moves with its King in the corner and the white Queen on g3. White cannot move the King closer because the game would end immediately in a stalemate.

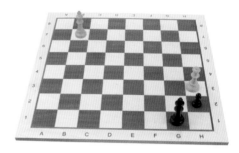

ANOTHER EXCEPTION

It would appear again that white will be able to bring the King on a6 closer and closer to the pawn. However, black has an important move to play. White begins by moving its King closer to the action with Ka6-b5. Black responds by moving its King toward the corner with Kf1-g1.

In order to try to prevent black from Queening the pawn, white plays Qf3-g3+, expecting that black will move its King back in front of the f2-pawn. Instead, black cleverly moves the King into the h1 corner.

CONTINUED ON NEXT PAGE

White cannot capture the pawn because that position is a stalemate! Any King move would permit black to Queen the pawn. There's simply no way to make progress.

The Exception to the Exception

The difference in this position is that the white King is already just close enough to enter the action. White begins with Qh3-g3+. Hoping for a stalemate, black responds with Kg1-h1.

Rather than bring the King up closer, white releases the black King out of the corner with Qg3-f3+. The King is forced to return to the g1 square.

White could easily repeat the position with Qf3-g3+, but white has the surprising Kd4-e3. Black could delay the game a bit by promoting the pawn to a Knight. (I will leave it to you to see if you can force the checkmate quickly in that position.) Here, black prefers to promote the pawn to a Queen.

The game ends beautifully with Qf3-f2 checkmate. The new Queen blocks the King's retreat back into the corner! As you can see, a Knight on h1 would have prevented this checkmate by guarding the f2-square.

Glossary of Chess Terms

Check notation.

+   Checkmate notation.

++   Double checkmate notation.

?   Bad move notation.

??   Very bad move notation.

algebraic notation   A method for recording chess moves that uses the letters a–h to describe the board's *ranks* and the numbers 1–8 to describe the board's *files*. The letters K, Q, R, B, N describe each of the pieces. The notation Ng1-f3 describes the movement of the Knight from g1 to f3.

attack   An aggressive move or set of moves aimed at winning material or delivering checkmate to the enemy King.

back rank mate   A Rook or Queen checks the enemy King along the back rank, and the King's escape is blocked by its own pawn.

bad Bishop   A Bishop with limited mobility due to its own pawns being fixed on its color.

capture   A capture is the movement of a piece onto the square occupied by an enemy piece. That enemy piece is immediately removed from the board.

castling   The only move in chess that moves two pieces, the King and Rook, at the same time. The King moves two squares toward the Rook. The Rook is then moved to the other side of the King. To castle, the King and Rook must not have previously moved. You cannot castle out of, through, or into check.

center   The squares d4, e4, d5, and e5 comprise the center. The squares immediately surrounding these four squares are sometimes included in the definition. In the opening phase of the game, both players often fight for control over these key squares.

check   A check is a move that attacks a King. On the very next move, the King must end the attack, either by moving to a safe square, capturing the attacking piece, or by blocking the attack. Note that you are not required to say "check."

checkmate   The end of a chess game occurs when there is an attack on a King (a check) from which there is no escape. Note that the King is not actually removed from the board.

correspondence chess   A form of chess in which two players compete through the mail. Today, e-mail chess is becoming as or more popular than postal chess—the sending of post cards that contain chess moves.

diagonals   The chessboard has alternating black and white squares. The white and black squares form diagonals that cut through the board. Some of the diagonals are longer than others. Placing a Bishop on the longest diagonals, for example the diagonal stretching from a1 through h8, can increase their scope.

discovered checks   You move a piece, which exposes an attack from the piece behind it.

double check   When moving a piece exposes a check from behind it, while the piece itself also gives check.

draw   A completed chess game that has no winner. Both players can agree to a draw at any time. See also definition of *stalemate* on page *275*. Other types of draws are discussed in Chapter 2, "Special Moves."

en passant   When a pawn moves forward two squares, a pawn on an adjacent file can capture, only on its next move, the pawn as if it had moved forward only one square. The rule was introduced to make sure that a pawn could not advance all the way down the board without an adjacent pawn having an opportunity to capture it.

endgame   The final phase of the game, often distinguished by a simplified amount of material.

fianchetto   A pawn structure that permits a player to place a Bishop quickly on one of the board's long diagonals. For example, advancing a pawn from g2 to g3 permits white to continue with Bf1-g2, fianchettoing white's light-squared Bishop.

file   The chessboard contains eight vertical columns or files. In chess, we identify each file with a different letter, a–h. And so, white's left-most file is the a-file; the right-most file is the h-file.

flanks   Files that are on the outside edges of the board (a, b, g, or h files).

fork   An attack, usually by Knight, on two enemy pieces at the same time. Forks of more than two pieces are called *family forks*.

gambit   A gambit is a move or an opening that offers a pawn or more in exchange for control over the center, a file, or a key square. The most famous opening gambits are the *King's Gambit* (1.e2-e4 e7-e4 2.f2-f4) and the *Queen's Gambit* (1.d2-d4 d7-d5 2.c2-c4).

good Bishop   A Bishop that is able to attack the opponent's fixed pawns (pawns that are unable to move).

illegal move   A move that is in violation of the laws of chess. When discovered, the game should be returned to the exact point that the illegal move occurred. The player who made the illegal move must then make a legal move with the piece that was moved illegally.

Kingside   The Kingside refers to the area on the side of the board on which the King began the game. On white's side of the board, for example, the term usually refers to the squares f1, g1, h1, f2, g2, h2, and f3, g3, h3. The expression, attacking white's Kingside, will usually refer to a piece- or pawn-led attack on at least one of those squares.

Knight fork   An attack by a Knight on two or more pieces at the same time.

middlegame   The phase of a chess game after the opening in which both sides use their developed pieces to contest important squares or regions of the board and begin to attack each other's King positions.

passed pawn   A pawn that no longer must face enemy pawns as it advances toward its Queening square.

pawn chain   A group of pawns set along a diagonal. The weakest pawn is the pawn in the rear of the chain because none of the other pawns can defend it. Most players, therefore, attack pawn chains at the weakest point, the pawn in the rear of the chain.

perpetual check   A never ending series of checks.

pin   There are two types of pins. An *absolute pin* is an attack on a piece that cannot now move because doing so would expose an attack on the King. A *relative pin* is an attack on a piece that can legally move, but doing so would expose an attack on a powerful and more valuable piece like the Queen.

Queening square   The square on the eighth rank on which a pawn, having reached it, will promote from a pawn to a Knight, Bishop, Rook, or Queen. Most players promote to a Queen, the most powerful piece. Hence the name.

Queenside   The Queenside refers to the area on the side of the board on which the Queen began the game. On white's side of the board, for example, the term usually refers to the squares a1, b1, c1, a2, b2, c2, and a3, b3, c3. The expression, attacking white's Queenside, will usually refer to a piece- or pawn-led attack on at least one of those squares.

rank   The chessboard contains eight horizontal rows or ranks. In chess, we identify each rank with a different number, 1–8. And so, white's bottom-most rank is the first rank. White's top-most rank is the eighth rank.

skewer   An attack on a piece that results, after the retreat of the attacked piece, in the win of a more distant piece along that same rank, file, or diagonal.

stalemate   A special situation in which a player has no legal moves anywhere on the board, and the King is not in check. The result is a draw.

United States Chess Federation   The official governing body of American chess. Visit their website at www.uschess.org.

Index

by Knight, 8, 15
notation for, 17–18
by pawns, 8, 16, 78–79, 98–99
by Queen, 8, 14, 83
by Rook, 8, 12
moves. *See also specific formations and strategies*
and 50-move rule, 27, 184
opening, 9
planning, 153–159
threats contained in, 160
My 60 Most Memorable Games (Bobby Fischer), 140
My System (Aron Nimzovitsch), 148

N

Nimzo-Indian Defense, 128
Nimzovitsch, Aron
Blockade, 148
and five steps to victory, 148–152
and French Winawer, 141
and Nimzo-Indian Defense, 128
notation, chess
check in, 190
described, 17–18
double check in, 190
white preceding black moves in, 102

O

1001 Brilliant Ways to Checkmate (Fred Reinfeld), 140
online games, 95, 145, 152
open files
checkmate by Rooks in, 41
moving Rooks to, 38–39
opening formation
Avant-Garde, 138
Benoni, 144–145
Colle System, 135
Dragon, 139–140
French Winawer, 141–142
Hedgehog, 136–137
King's Indian Attack, 132–134
online, 145
Stonewall, 143
opening move, 9
opening strategy
avoiding exchange of Bishops for Knights, 107
developing Bishops first, 97
developing completely before attacking, 100–101

fighting for center of board, 92–93
gaining time, 102
ideal setup, 94–95
Knights before Bishops, 96–97
limiting early pawn moves, 98–99
limiting exchanges, 103–106
most common, 92–93
opening variation(s)
Alekhine's Defense, 121–122
bad, 129
Caro-Kann Defense, 120–121
Center Game, 113
double King pawn, 110–117
double Queen pawn, 123–125
Englund Gambit, 129
French Defense, 119
Indian Defenses, 126–128
King's Gambit, 110
King's Indian Defense, 126
Nimzo-Indian Defense, 128
Petrov's Defense, 115–117
Queen's Gambit, 123
Queen's Gambit Declined, 124
Queen's Indian Defense, 127
Ruy Lopez, 113–114
Scotch game, 115
Sicilian Defense, 118
Slav Defense, 125
Spike, 129
Vienna Game, 111–112
outpost, 257

P

passed pawn
blockading, 77
defined, 43
endgame with single Bishop and, 257–260
Rooks behind, 43
pawn(s). *See also specific strategies*
advancing, in front of castled King, 88–89
attacking weakness with, 150
avoiding attacks on Knights by, 48
backward, 71
capture by, 8, 16
described, 8
doubled, 64, 66
double King pawn openings, 110–117

Teach Yourself VISUALLY™ books...

Whether you want to knit, sew, or crochet...strum a guitar or play the piano...train a dog or create a scrapbook...make the most of Windows XP or touch up your Photoshop CS2 skills, Teach Yourself VISUALLY books get you into action instead of bogging you down in lengthy instructions. All Teach Yourself VISUALLY books are written by experts on the subject and feature:

- Hundreds of color photos or screenshots that demonstrate each step or skill

- Step-by-step instructions accompanying each photo
- FAQs that answer common questions and suggest solutions to common problems
- Information about each skill clearly presented on a two- or four-page spread so you can learn by seeing and doing
- A design that makes it easy to review a particular topic

Look for Teach Yourself VISUALLY books to help you learn a variety of skills—all with the proven visual learning approaches you enjoyed in this book.

0-7645-9641-1

Teach Yourself VISUALLY™ Crocheting

Picture yourself crocheting accessories, garments, and great home décor items. It's a relaxing hobby, and this is the relaxing way to learn! This Visual guide *shows* you the basics, beginning with the tools and materials needed and the basic stitches, then progresses through following patterns, creating motifs and fun shapes, and finishing details. A variety of patterns gets you started, and more advanced patterns get you hooked!

0-7645-9640-3

Teach Yourself VISUALLY™ Knitting

Get yourself some yarn and needles and get clicking! This Visual guide *shows* you the basics of knitting—photo by photo and stitch by stitch. You begin with the basic knit and purl patterns and advance to bobbles, knots, cables, openwork, and finishing techniques—knitting as you go. With fun, innovative patterns from top designer Sharon Turner, you'll be creating masterpieces in no time!

0-7645-9642-X

Teach Yourself VISUALLY™ Guitar

Pick up this book and a guitar and start strumming! *Teach Yourself VISUALLY Guitar* shows you the basics photo by photo and note by note. You begin with essential chords and techniques and progress through suspensions, bass runs, hammer-ons, and barre chords. As you learn to read chord charts, tablature, and lead sheets, you can play any number of songs, from rock to folk to country. The chord chart and scale appendices are ready references for use long after you master the basics.

designed for visual learners like you!

0-7645-7927-4

Teach Yourself VISUALLY™ Windows® XP, 2nd Edition

Clear step-by-step screenshots *show* you how to tackle more than 150 Windows XP tasks. Learn how to draw, fill, and edit shapes, set up and secure an Internet account, load images from a digital camera, copy tracks from music CDs, defragment your hard drive, and more.

0-7645-8840-0

Teach Yourself VISUALLY™ Photoshop® CS2

Clear step-by-step screenshots *show* you how to tackle more than 150 Photoshop CS2 tasks. Learn how to import images from digital cameras, repair damaged photos, browse and sort images in Bridge, change image size and resolution, paint and draw with color, create duotone images, apply layer and filter effects, and more.

Available wherever books are sold.

Visual®
An Imprint of ⑂**WILEY**
Now you know.